DIN ASOTIC

Mastering API

A Comprehensive Guide to Building and Integrating APIs

Contents

III   Building a RESTful API

VII   API Testing and Monitoring

I

Introduction to APIs

1

What is an API?

An Application Programming Interface (API) is a set of rules, protocols, and tools that enables different software applications to communicate with each other. In essence, an API acts as a bridge between two software programs, allowing them to share data and functionality. The term API can refer to both the specifications and the actual implementation of these communication rules.

APIs have become a fundamental aspect of modern software development, enabling developers to create new applications by utilizing existing resources, services, and data. In this chapter, we will explore the concept of APIs, their primary components, and the benefits they provide to software developers.

API Components

APIs consist of several essential components, which together facilitate communication between software applications. These components include:

Specifications and Protocols

API specifications outline the rules and protocols that dictate how applications should interact with one another. These rules govern various aspects of communication, such as data formats, methods, and conventions. Common API protocols include REST, SOAP, and GraphQL, each with its unique set of specifications.

Endpoints

API endpoints are the specific points of interaction between applications. Endpoints define the location where requests are sent and where responses are received. Each endpoint typically corresponds to a specific function or resource within the API, such as retrieving data, updating data, or deleting data.

Methods

API methods, also known as HTTP verbs, define the actions that can be performed on a resource. Common methods include GET (retrieve data), POST (create new data), PUT (update existing data), and DELETE (remove data). These methods enable applications to interact with the API in a standardized way.

Data Formats

APIs use specific data formats to structure the data exchanged between applications. The most common data format used in APIs is JSON (JavaScript Object Notation), a lightweight, text-based format that is easy to read and write. Other data formats include XML (Extensible Markup Language) and YAML (YAML Ain't Markup Language).

Authentication and Authorization

APIs often require authentication and authorization mechanisms to ensure that only authorized users can access the resources and perform actions. These mechanisms include API keys, OAuth, and JSON Web Tokens (JWT), which help protect the API from unauthorized access and potential security threats.

Types of APIs

APIs can be classified into several categories based on their purpose, scope, and architectural style. Some common types of APIs include:

Web APIs

Web APIs, also known as Web Services, are APIs that enable communication between applications over the internet. They use standard internet protocols such as HTTP and HTTPS for data transmission. Web APIs can be further categorized based on their architectural style, such as REST, SOAP, and GraphQL.

Library and Framework APIs

Library and Framework APIs are sets of pre-built functions and tools that developers can use to build their applications. They provide a consistent and standardized way to access functionality, speeding up development and reducing potential errors. Examples include the Java Standard Library, the .NET Framework, and the Ruby on Rails framework.

Operating System APIs

Operating System APIs allow applications to interact with the underlying operating system, enabling developers to perform tasks such as file management, network communication, and process control. Examples of operating system APIs include the Windows API, macOS Cocoa, and the Linux POSIX API.

Hardware APIs

Hardware APIs provide a standardized interface for interacting with physical devices and peripherals. They abstract the complexities of hardware communication, enabling developers to build applications that can interact with hardware devices without needing to understand their low-level details. Examples of hardware APIs include USB (Universal Serial Bus) API, Bluetooth API, and GPU (Graphics Processing Unit) APIs.

The Role of APIs in Software Development

APIs have become an integral part of modern software development, enabling developers to leverage existing resources, services, and data to create new applications. Some of the key roles that APIs play in software development include:

Reusability and Modularity

APIs promote reusability and modularity by encapsulating functionality within discrete, well-defined interfaces. This allows developers to build applications more efficiently by utilizing pre-built components and services. APIs also enable the separation of concerns, making it easier to maintain and update individual components without affecting the entire application.

Integration and Interoperability

APIs enable applications to interact with one another, facilitating seamless integration and interoperability. This allows developers to create new applications by combining existing services, data, and functionality from different sources. For example, a weather application can use an API to access real-time weather data from a third-party provider, or a social media application can use an API to authenticate users and access their profile information.

Extensibility and Customization

APIs provide a standardized interface for extending and customizing applications, allowing developers to create new features and modify existing ones without needing to modify the underlying codebase. This enables a more flexible and adaptable development process, as well as promoting a more sustainable and maintainable application architecture.

Abstraction and Simplification

APIs abstract the complexities of underlying systems and services, providing a simplified interface for developers to interact with. This enables developers to focus on building their applications without needing to understand the low-level details of the systems they are interacting with. APIs also help to reduce the learning curve associated with using new technologies and services, making it easier for developers to adopt and integrate them into their applications.

The Benefits of Using APIs

APIs provide numerous benefits to developers, businesses, and end-users. Some of the key advantages of using APIs include:

Faster Development

APIs enable developers to build applications more quickly by utilizing pre-built components and services. This reduces the time and effort required to develop new features, as well as minimizing the potential for errors and inconsistencies.

Cost Savings

APIs can lead to cost savings by allowing businesses to leverage existing resources, services, and data, rather than investing in the development of new solutions. Additionally, APIs can reduce maintenance costs by promoting modularity and separation of concerns, making it easier to update and maintain individual components.

Scalability

APIs facilitate the development of scalable applications by allowing developers to easily integrate with existing services and infrastructure. This enables applications to grow and adapt to changing requirements and demands, ensuring they can continue to meet the needs of users and businesses.

Innovation and Collaboration

APIs enable innovation and collaboration by providing a standardized interface for developers to access and share data, functionality, and resources. This promotes the development of new applications and services, as well as fostering collaboration between different organizations and development teams.

Improved User Experience

APIs can lead to an improved user experience by enabling applications to access real-time data, functionality, and services from various sources. This allows developers to create more dynamic, responsive, and feature-rich applications that better meet the needs and expectations of users.

APIs are a fundamental aspect of modern software development, allowing applications to communicate and share data, functionality, and resources. They promote reusability, modularity, and integration, enabling developers to build more efficient, scalable, and innovative applications. APIs also provide numerous benefits, including cost savings, faster development, and improved user experiences. As the demand for interconnected and data-driven applications continues to grow, the importance of APIs in software development will only increase.

2

Types of APIs

There are various types of APIs, each serving different purposes and catering to specific needs within software development. Some common types of APIs include Web APIs, Library and Framework APIs, Operating System APIs, and Hardware APIs. Each of these API types has its unique characteristics, advantages, and use cases, which will be discussed in greater detail throughout this book.

REST

Representational State Transfer (REST) is an architectural style for designing networked applications. RESTful APIs, also known as REST APIs, are built on this architectural style and have become a popular choice for developing Web APIs due to their simplicity, scalability, and ease of use. In this section, we will explore the principles of REST, its key components, and the benefits it offers in designing APIs.

Principles of REST

REST is based on a set of guiding principles that dictate how applications should interact and exchange data over a network. These principles include:

Stateless

REST requires that each request from a client to a server must contain all the necessary information for the server to process the request. The server should not store any information about the client's state between requests, which promotes greater scalability and simplifies the server's implementation.

Cacheable

Responses from the server can be cached by the client to improve performance and reduce the load on the server. Proper cache management is essential for ensuring that clients receive up-to-date and accurate data while minimizing the number of requests made to the server.

Client-Server Architecture

REST is based on a client-server architecture, where the client is responsible for the user interface and the server is responsible for processing requests and managing resources. This separation of concerns allows for greater flexibility and easier development, as the client and server can evolve independently of one another.

Layered System

REST promotes a layered system architecture, where each layer has a specific responsibility and is only aware of the layers directly adjacent to it. This abstraction helps to simplify the overall system, making it easier to understand, maintain, and update.

Uniform Interface

A key aspect of REST is the uniform interface, which standardizes the way clients and servers communicate with one another. This uniformity simplifies the overall architecture, making it easier to understand, develop, and maintain. The uniform interface consists of several constraints, such as using standard HTTP methods, providing self-descriptive messages, and utilizing resource identifiers (URIs) to address resources.

Components of RESTful APIs

RESTful APIs consist of several key components that facilitate communication between clients and servers. These components include:

Resources

In REST, resources are the primary abstraction and represent any object or entity that can be identified and manipulated via the API. Resources are typically accessed and modified using standard HTTP methods (GET, POST, PUT, DELETE) and are addressed using unique resource identifiers (URIs).

HTTP Methods

RESTful APIs use standard HTTP methods to perform actions on resources. These methods include GET (retrieve a resource), POST (create a new resource), PUT (update an existing resource), and DELETE (remove a resource). By adhering to these standard methods, RESTful APIs provide a consistent and intuitive interface for interacting with resources.

URIs

Unique Resource Identifiers (URIs) are used to address and identify resources within a RESTful API. URIs provide a simple and consistent way to access resources, making it easy for clients to interact with the API. Well-designed URIs should be self-explanatory and hierarchical, allowing clients to understand the structure and relationships between resources.

Representations

In RESTful APIs, resources can have multiple representations, such as JSON, XML, or YAML. These representations are used to convey the state of a resource and facilitate the exchange of data between the client and server. Clients can request specific representations using the "Accept" header in their HTTP request, while servers can indicate the representation used in the response using the "Content-Type" header.

Hypermedia as the Engine of Application State (HATEOAS)

HATEOAS is an optional constraint of RESTful APIs that promotes the discoverability of resources and actions by including hypermedia links within representations. These links allow clients to navigate the API and perform actions on resources without prior knowledge of the URI structure. HATEOAS helps to create more flexible and maintainable APIs by decoupling the client and server implementations.

Benefits of RESTful APIs

RESTful APIs offer several benefits that make them a popular choice for designing Web APIs. Some of these benefits include:

Simplicity

RESTful APIs are built on the foundation of the existing HTTP protocol, making them simple and easy to understand. Developers can leverage their existing knowledge of HTTP methods, status codes, and headers to create and consume RESTful APIs with minimal learning curve.

Scalability

The stateless nature of RESTful APIs promotes greater scalability, as servers do not need to maintain session information for clients. This allows servers to handle a larger number of simultaneous connections and reduces the resources required to process requests.

Cacheability

RESTful APIs support caching of responses, which can improve performance and reduce the load on servers. By allowing clients to cache and reuse data, RESTful APIs can help minimize network traffic and decrease response times.

Interoperability

RESTful APIs are platform and language agnostic, making them highly interoperable across different systems and technologies. Clients can be built using any programming language or platform, as long as they can send and receive HTTP requests and process the resource representations.

Evolvability

The uniform interface and layered architecture of RESTful APIs make it easier to evolve and maintain APIs over time. Changes to the underlying implementation or the addition of new features can be made without impacting existing clients, as long as the API's interface remains consistent.

In conclusion, RESTful APIs are a popular choice for designing Web APIs due to their simplicity, scalability, and ease of use. By adhering to the principles and components of REST, developers can create APIs that are flexible, maintainable, and interoperable across different systems and technologies. As the demand for data-driven applications and services continues to grow, RESTful APIs will play a crucial role in enabling seamless communication and integration between applications.

GraphQL

GraphQL is a query language and runtime for APIs, developed by Facebook in 2012 and released as an open-source project in 2015. It offers a flexible and efficient approach to requesting and modifying data, allowing clients to request exactly what they need and nothing more. In this section, we will explore the features and principles of GraphQL, its key components, and the benefits it offers in designing APIs.

Features and Principles of GraphQL

GraphQL is built on a set of core features and principles that aim to address some of the limitations of traditional RESTful APIs. These features include:

Declarative Data Fetching

In GraphQL, clients specify the data they need by describing their requirements in a query. This allows clients to request only the data they need, reducing the amount of over- or under-fetching and optimizing network usage.

Hierarchical Data

GraphQL organizes data in a hierarchical structure, which reflects the relationships between different types of data in the application. This makes it easier for clients to request and understand the data they receive.

Strongly Typed

GraphQL is a strongly typed language, which means that every piece of data has a specific type associated with it. This enables better error handling and validation, as well as providing a clear contract between the client and server.

Introspective

GraphQL APIs are introspective, which means that clients can query the schema to learn about the available types, fields, and relationships. This enables dynamic clients to adapt to changes in the API without requiring hard-coded knowledge of the schema.

Single Endpoint

In contrast to RESTful APIs, which typically have multiple endpoints for different resources, GraphQL APIs expose a single endpoint for all data and operations. This simplifies the client-server interaction and makes it easier to manage and maintain the API.

Components of GraphQL APIs

GraphQL APIs consist of several key components that facilitate communication between clients and servers. These components include:

Schema

The schema is the heart of a GraphQL API and defines the types, fields, and relationships available to clients. It serves as a contract between the client and server, specifying the data that can be requested and the operations that can be performed. The schema is written using the GraphQL Schema Definition Language (SDL).

23

Queries

Queries are the primary means of requesting data in a GraphQL API. Clients construct queries by specifying the fields and relationships they need, as well as any arguments or filters to apply. The server processes the query and returns the requested data in a JSON format.

Mutations

Mutations are the counterpart to queries and are used to modify data in a GraphQL API. Mutations allow clients to create, update, and delete data, as well as perform other side effects such as sending emails or triggering notifications. Like queries, mutations are defined in the schema and can accept arguments to specify the changes to be made.

Resolvers

Resolvers are the functions responsible for fetching or modifying data in response to queries and mutations. They are responsible for implementing the logic required to access and manipulate the underlying data sources, such as databases or external APIs. Resolvers are typically written in the same language as the server implementation, such as JavaScript, Python, or Ruby.

Subscriptions

Subscriptions enable real-time updates and event-driven communication between clients and servers in a GraphQL API. Clients can subscribe to specific events or data updates, allowing them to receive notifications when changes occur. This can be useful for applications that require real-time data synchronization, such as chat applications or dashboards.

Benefits of GraphQL APIs

GraphQL offers several benefits over traditional RESTful APIs, making it an attractive option for many developers and organizations. Some of these benefits include:

Flexibility

GraphQL's declarative approach to data fetching allows clients to request exactly what they need and nothing more.

This reduces the amount of over- or under-fetching and optimizes network usage, which is particularly important for mobile and low-bandwidth environments.

Strong Typing

The strongly typed nature of GraphQL enables better error handling and validation, as well as providing a clear contract between the client and server. This can lead to fewer errors and more robust APIs, as well as improved developer experience and tooling.

Introspection

The introspective capabilities of GraphQL APIs allow clients to query the schema to learn about the available types, fields, and relationships. This enables dynamic clients to adapt to changes in the API without requiring hard-coded knowledge of the schema, resulting in more maintainable and adaptable applications.

Real-Time Updates

With the addition of subscriptions, GraphQL APIs can support real-time updates and event-driven communication. This is valuable for applications that require live data synchronization or notifications, such as chat applications, collaboration tools, or real-time analytics dashboards.

Simplified API Management

By exposing a single endpoint for all data and operations, GraphQL APIs simplify the client-server interaction and make it easier to manage and maintain the API. This can lead to reduced development complexity and improved maintainability over time.

In conclusion, GraphQL is a powerful and flexible alternative to traditional RESTful APIs, offering a range of benefits and features that can help developers build more efficient, adaptable, and maintainable applications. By embracing the core principles and components of GraphQL, developers can create APIs that better serve the needs of their clients and adapt to the evolving requirements of modern applications. As the demand for more sophisticated data-driven applications continues to grow, GraphQL is poised to play a significant role in the future of API design and development.

SOAP

Simple Object Access Protocol (SOAP) is a messaging protocol for exchanging structured information between web services in a distributed and decentralized environment. Initially developed by Microsoft in the late 1990s, SOAP has been a cornerstone of web service communication for many years, particularly in enterprise settings. In this section, we will explore the features and principles of SOAP, its key components, and the benefits it offers in designing APIs.

Features and Principles of SOAP

SOAP is built on a set of core features and principles that aim to facilitate communication between web services in a standardized and reliable manner. These features include:

Extensibility

SOAP is designed to be extensible, allowing developers to add features and functionality to the protocol as needed. This is achieved through the use of XML namespaces and modular structure, which enables SOAP to evolve and adapt to the changing requirements of web services.

Neutrality

SOAP is transport-neutral, meaning it can be used with various communication protocols such as HTTP, SMTP, or TCP. This enables SOAP-based web services to be accessible across different platforms and environments, increasing their interoperability and flexibility.

Independence

SOAP is language and platform-independent, allowing developers to create and consume web services using any programming language or platform that supports XML processing. This ensures that SOAP-based web services can be used by a wide range of clients and servers, further enhancing their interoperability.

Reliability

SOAP includes built-in features for enhancing the reliability of web service communication, such as support for message retries and acknowledgements. This helps to ensure that messages are successfully delivered between web services, even in the face of network failures or other disruptions.

Components of SOAP APIs

SOAP APIs consist of several key components that facilitate communication between web services. These components include:

SOAP Messages

SOAP messages are the primary means of communication between web services and are composed of an XML document that follows a specific structure. The structure includes a SOAP envelope, which contains a header and a body. The header can include metadata and additional information about the message, while the body contains the actual data being exchanged.

SOAP Operations

SOAP operations are the actions that can be performed by a SOAP-based web service. These operations are defined using a Web Services Description Language (WSDL) document, which provides a machine-readable description of the web service's interface. Clients can use the WSDL document to understand the available operations, their input and output parameters, and the data types involved.

XML Namespaces

XML namespaces are used in SOAP messages to distinguish between different elements and attributes that may have the same name. This is particularly important in SOAP because it allows for the protocol to be extensible and adaptable to different use cases and environments.

Fault Handling

SOAP includes built-in support for error handling and reporting through the use of SOAP faults. A SOAP fault is a special type of message that can be returned by a web service to indicate that an error has occurred during the processing of a request. Faults include information about the nature of the error, allowing clients to handle and recover from errors more effectively.

Benefits of SOAP APIs

SOAP APIs offer several benefits that make them a popular choice for certain use cases and environments, particularly in enterprise settings. Some of these benefits include:

Standardization

SOAP is a widely adopted and standardized protocol for web service communication, providing a common framework for exchanging information between disparate systems. This standardization enables greater interoperability and makes it easier to integrate web services developed by different organizations or using different technologies.

Extensibility

The extensible nature of SOAP allows developers to add features and functionality to the protocol as needed. This enables SOAP-based web services to evolve and adapt to the changing requirements of their users and environments, ensuring that they remain relevant and useful over time.

Platform and Language Independence

SOAP's platform and language independence ensure that web services can be developed and consumed using any programming language or platform that supports XML processing. This broadens the potential user base for SOAP-based web services and enables greater flexibility and choice for developers.

Reliability

The built-in features for enhancing reliability in SOAP, such as message retries and acknowledgements, help to ensure that messages are successfully delivered between web services, even in the face of network failures or other disruptions. This can be particularly important in mission-critical applications or environments where the reliability of communication is paramount.

Security

SOAP provides a range of security features, such as support for message encryption and digital signatures, that can help protect the confidentiality and integrity of web service communication. These features can be important for applications that deal with sensitive or confidential information, as well as for ensuring compliance with security regulations and standards.

In conclusion, SOAP is a mature and standardized protocol for web service communication that offers a range of benefits for certain use cases and environments. Its extensibility, platform independence, and built-in reliability features make it well-suited for enterprise applications and other scenarios where the integration of disparate systems is a key requirement. However, the increasing popularity of more lightweight and flexible alternatives, such as REST and GraphQL, has led to a decline in the use of SOAP for new API development. Despite this, SOAP remains an important and relevant technology for many existing applications and will continue to play a role in the broader API landscape.

3

API Terminology

I n this chapter, we will explore the most common terminology used when discussing APIs. Familiarizing yourself with these terms will help you better understand the concepts discussed throughout this book and communicate more effectively with other developers and stakeholders involved in API development and consumption.

API (Application Programming Interface)

An API (Application Programming Interface) is a set of rules, protocols, and tools that enables software applications to communicate with each other. APIs define the types of requests that can be made, the data that can be exchanged, and the conventions that must be followed when interacting with a software component or service.

API Endpoint

An API endpoint is a specific location or URL where requests can be sent and responses can be received. In RESTful APIs, each endpoint represents a specific resource or operation, while in GraphQL APIs, there is typically a single endpoint for all data and operations.

API Key

An API key is a unique identifier used for authentication and authorization purposes when accessing an API. API keys are often used to control access to an API, limit usage, or track the activity of individual developers or applications.

API Gateway

An API gateway is a server that acts as an intermediary between API clients and the services that provide the API. API gateways are responsible for handling API requests, managing authentication and authorization, and providing additional functionality such as rate limiting, caching, and logging.

API Versioning

API versioning is the practice of maintaining multiple versions of an API to accommodate changes in functionality or design. Versioning can help to prevent breaking changes for existing API clients while allowing for the introduction of new features and improvements.

Authentication

Authentication is the process of verifying the identity of a user, client, or server attempting to access an API. Common methods of authentication include API keys, OAuth tokens, or username and password combinations.

Authorization

Authorization is the process of determining what actions or resources a user, client, or server is allowed to access within an API. Authorization is typically managed through the use of access tokens, permissions, or roles.

Cache

A cache is a temporary storage mechanism that holds data or the results of API requests to improve performance and reduce the load on the API server. Caching can be implemented at various levels, including the client, server, or intermediate layers such as a content delivery network (CDN) or API gateway.

Client

In the context of APIs, a client is a software application or component that makes requests to an API to access or manipulate data. Clients can be web browsers, mobile apps, server applications, or other software components that interact with an API.

CORS (Cross-Origin Resource Sharing)

CORS (Cross-Origin Resource Sharing) is a security mechanism that allows web browsers to request resources from different domains. CORS is often used in APIs to enable web applications hosted on different domains to access data from the API without violating the same-origin policy.

CRUD (Create, Read, Update, Delete)

CRUD (Create, Read, Update, Delete) is a common set of operations used to interact with data in an API. These operations correspond to the actions of creating new resources, retrieving existing resources, updating resources, and deleting resources.

Data Model

A data model is a representation of the structure and relationships between different types of data in an application or API. Data models can be defined using various languages or notations, such as JSON Schema, GraphQL SDL, or XML Schema.

Documentation

API documentation is a detailed description of an API's functionality, including information about its endpoints, operations, data types, and usage guidelines. Documentation is an essential resource for developers and other stakeholders who need to understand how to use and interact with an API.

Error Handling

Error handling refers to the process of managing and reporting errors that occur during the execution of API requests. This can involve returning error messages, status codes, or other information to help clients identify and resolve issues.

GraphQL

GraphQL is a query language and runtime for APIs developed by Facebook. It allows clients to request specific data from an API, minimizing over- or under-fetching of data and optimizing network usage.

Header

An HTTP header is a piece of metadata included in an HTTP request or response. Headers can be used to provide additional information about the request or response, such as content type, caching settings, or authentication credentials.

HTTP (Hypertext Transfer Protocol)

HTTP (Hypertext Transfer Protocol) is the underlying protocol used by the World Wide Web for transmitting and receiving data. In the context of APIs, HTTP is often used as the communication protocol between clients and servers.

JSON (JavaScript Object Notation)

JSON (JavaScript Object Notation) is a lightweight data interchange format that is easy for humans to read and write and easy for machines to parse and generate. JSON is often used as the data format for APIs, as it is widely supported by modern programming languages and platforms.

Middleware

Middleware is a software component that sits between the client and server in an API and can be used to process or modify requests and responses. Middleware can be used for tasks such as authentication, logging, caching, or transforming data.

OAuth

OAuth is an open standard for authorization that allows users to grant third-party applications access to their data without sharing their credentials. OAuth is commonly used in APIs to provide a secure and standardized method for authenticating and authorizing clients.

Pagination

Pagination is the process of dividing large sets of data into smaller, more manageable chunks or "pages." Pagination is often used in APIs to improve performance and reduce the amount of data returned in a single request.

Payload

The payload is the data sent in the body of an HTTP request or response. In the context of APIs, the payload often contains the data being sent or received, such as the details of a resource or the results of a query.

Rate Limiting

Rate limiting is a technique used to control the rate at which clients can make requests to an API. Rate limiting can help protect an API from excessive usage or abuse and ensure fair access to resources.

REST (Representational State Transfer)

REST (Representational State Transfer) is an architectural style for designing networked applications that emphasizes scalability, simplicity, and the use of standard HTTP methods. RESTful APIs are designed around the principles of REST and use HTTP methods to perform CRUD operations on resources.

SDK (Software Development Kit)

An SDK (Software Development Kit) is a collection of software tools, libraries, and documentation that helps developers build applications for a specific platform or service. SDKs are often provided by API providers to make it easier for developers to interact with their APIs using specific programming languages or platforms.

SOAP (Simple Object Access Protocol)

SOAP (Simple Object Access Protocol) is a messaging protocol for exchanging structured information between web services in a distributed and decentralized environment. SOAP is an XML-based protocol that is often used in enterprise settings for web service communication.

Status Code

An HTTP status code is a numerical value returned by an HTTP server to indicate the outcome of an HTTP request. Status codes are used to communicate the success or failure of a request, as well as provide additional information about the request or response.

URI (Uniform Resource Identifier)

A URI (Uniform Resource Identifier) is a string of characters that identifies a name or a resource on the Internet. URIs are used in APIs to uniquely identify resources and provide a means of locating them within the API.

URL (Uniform Resource Locator)

A URL (Uniform Resource Locator) is a type of URI that specifies the location of a resource on the Internet and the protocol used to access it. In the context of APIs, URLs are often used as the addresses for API endpoints.

Webhook

A webhook is a mechanism for an API to send real-time notifications to a client or another server when a specific event or change occurs. Webhooks are typically implemented as HTTP callbacks, where the API sends an HTTP request to a predefined URL when the event is triggered.

WSDL (Web Services Description Language)

WSDL (Web Services Description Language) is an XML-based language used to describe the functionality offered by a web service, including its operations, input and output parameters, and data types. WSDL documents are used by clients to understand the available operations and the format of the messages required to interact with a SOAP-based web service.

XML (eXtensible Markup Language)

XML (eXtensible Markup Language) is a markup language used for encoding documents in a format that is both human-readable and machine-readable. XML is often used as the data format for SOAP-based APIs, as well as for other data interchange and serialization purposes.

This chapter has provided an overview of the most common terminology used in the context of APIs. Familiarity with these terms will help you understand the various concepts and technologies discussed throughout this book, as well as communicate effectively with other developers, stakeholders, and API providers. As you continue to work with APIs, you will likely encounter additional terms and concepts specific to particular API technologies, protocols, or use cases. Developing a strong foundation in API terminology will enable you to more easily understand and adapt to these new concepts as you encounter them.

4

Benefits of Using APIs

APIs offer numerous benefits that have contributed to their widespread adoption in modern software development. These benefits can be grouped into several key areas:

Improved Efficiency and Productivity

APIs enable developers to easily access and integrate external data and services into their applications, reducing the need to build and maintain complex functionality from scratch. By leveraging pre-built APIs, developers can focus on their core business logic, accelerating development timelines and improving productivity.

Enhanced Interoperability

APIs provide a standardized way for disparate systems to communicate and exchange data, allowing for seamless integration between different applications, platforms, and technologies. This interoperability enables organizations to build more flexible and adaptable solutions, capable of meeting evolving business needs and supporting a wide range of use cases.

Scalability and Performance

APIs are designed to handle varying levels of demand and can often be scaled up or down as needed to accommodate fluctuations in usage. This scalability, combined with caching, load balancing, and other performance optimizations, helps ensure that APIs can deliver consistent and reliable performance even under heavy load.

Easier Maintenance and Upgrades

By abstracting the underlying implementation details of a service or component, APIs enable developers to modify or enhance their systems without impacting the clients that

48

consume them. This separation of concerns makes it easier to maintain and upgrade software over time, reducing the risk of breaking changes and minimizing the overall maintenance burden.

Increased Reusability and Modularity

APIs promote a modular approach to software development, where functionality is encapsulated in discrete, reusable components. This modularity not only improves the organization and maintainability of codebases but also encourages the reuse of existing functionality across multiple projects, reducing redundancy and promoting consistency.

Faster Innovation and Market Adoption

APIs facilitate the rapid development and deployment of new applications and services, enabling organizations to quickly bring new ideas to market and stay ahead of the competition. By providing access to a wealth of data, tools, and resources, APIs empower developers to innovate more quickly and drive the adoption of new technologies and business models.

Expanded Ecosystems and Partnerships

APIs make it easier for organizations to collaborate and form partnerships by providing a common interface for sharing data and functionality. By exposing their APIs to external developers, organizations can tap into a broader ecosystem of partners and customers, creating new revenue streams, and unlocking additional value from their existing assets.

Enhanced Security and Compliance

APIs provide a controlled and standardized way to access sensitive data and functionality, ensuring that security and compliance requirements can be more easily met. By implementing access controls, authentication, and other security measures at the API level, organizations can reduce the risk of data breaches and ensure that their systems remain secure and compliant.

In summary, APIs offer a multitude of benefits that have made them an essential tool in modern software development. By enabling greater efficiency, interoperability, scalability, and flexibility, APIs empower organizations to build more robust, adaptable, and innovative solutions that can meet the ever-changing demands of today's digital landscape.

5

Real-world API Examples

APIs have become integral to the modern digital landscape, powering countless applications and services that we interact with daily. In this section, we will explore several real-world examples of APIs, providing insight into their functionality, use cases, and how they have transformed the way businesses and developers build software.

Google Maps API

Google Maps API is a collection of APIs that enable developers to incorporate Google Maps features and data into their applications. These APIs provide access to various functionalities, including mapping, geolocation, route planning, and geocoding (translating addresses into geographic coordinates).

Use cases:

- Displaying a map within a website or mobile app, with custom markers and interactivity.
- Providing directions and route planning for users, taking into account various modes of transportation, such as driving, walking, or public transit.
- Searching for nearby points of interest, such as restaurants, hotels, or landmarks.
- Integrating geolocation features to track user locations and offer personalized experiences.

Impact: Google Maps API has revolutionized how businesses and developers incorporate location-based services into their applications. By providing easy access to accurate and up-to-date mapping data, it has enabled countless businesses to create location-aware services, improving user experiences and driving innovation in industries such as transportation, tourism, and real estate.

Twitter API

The Twitter API allows developers to access and interact with the vast amount of data available on the Twitter platform. This API provides a variety of endpoints for working with tweets, user profiles, trends, and more, enabling developers to build applications that consume, create, and analyze Twitter content.

Use cases:

- Building social media management tools that enable users to schedule, post, and monitor tweets across multiple accounts.
- Creating data visualization tools to analyze tweet patterns, sentiment, and trends in real-time.
- Developing chatbots or customer service applications that interact with users through tweets or direct messages.
- Aggregating and displaying curated Twitter content within websites, mobile apps, or other digital platforms.

Impact: The Twitter API has transformed the way businesses and developers engage with and leverage social media data. By providing programmatic access to the Twitter platform, it has enabled a wide range of innovative applications and services, from social media analytics tools to real-time news aggregators and social listening solutions.

Stripe API

The Stripe API is a payment processing API that allows businesses and developers to accept and manage online payments securely and efficiently. With its simple and well-documented API, Stripe has become a popular choice for developers looking to implement payment processing functionality in their applications.

Use cases:

- Enabling e-commerce websites and mobile apps to accept

credit card payments from customers.
· Facilitating recurring billing and subscription management for online services.
· Implementing marketplace functionality, allowing multiple vendors to accept payments within a single platform.
· Creating customized invoicing and payment solutions
tailored to specific business needs.

Impact: Stripe's API has streamlined the process of integrating payment processing into applications, reducing the complexity and security risks associated with handling sensitive
financial data. By providing a reliable, scalable, and developer-
friendly solution, Stripe has empowered businesses to create
seamless and secure payment experiences for their users,
driving growth in the global e-commerce and digital services
markets.

Spotify API

The Spotify API enables developers to access and interact with
Spotify's vast music catalog and user data. This API provides
various endpoints for searching, retrieving, and managing
information about artists, albums, tracks, playlists, and user
profiles.
Use cases:

· Developing music discovery applications that recommend
songs or artists based on user preferences or listening

history.

- Integrating Spotify playback functionality into websites, mobile apps, or other devices, allowing users to listen to music within a custom interface.
- Creating personalized playlists or radio stations by combining Spotify's music catalog with user data and third-party data sources.
- Building tools for analyzing and visualizing music trends, artist popularity, or other metadata related to the Spotify catalog.

Impact: The Spotify API has fueled innovation in the music and entertainment industries by providing developers with access to a vast library of music and user data. By enabling the creation of personalized and engaging music experiences, the API has helped drive the growth of the streaming music market and opened up new opportunities for artists, record labels, and other stakeholders within the industry.

Twilio API

Twilio is a cloud communications platform that offers APIs for voice, messaging, and video communication services. The Twilio API allows developers to programmatically send and receive text messages, make and receive phone calls, and facilitate video calls within their applications.

Use cases:

- Building SMS-based notification systems for sending alerts, updates, or reminders to users.
- Developing customer support applications that enable agents to call or text customers directly from a web-based interface.
- Creating two-factor authentication systems that leverage SMS or voice calls to verify user identities.
- Implementing video conferencing or real-time collaboration tools within web and mobile applications.

Impact: The Twilio API has transformed the way businesses communicate with their customers and users by providing an easy-to-use platform for integrating voice, messaging, and video services into applications. By removing the complexities of working with traditional telecommunication infrastructure, Twilio has empowered developers to create innovative communication solutions that improve customer engagement, support, and satisfaction.

Amazon Web Services (AWS) APIs

Amazon Web Services (AWS) is a suite of cloud-based infrastructure and platform services that provide APIs for various functionalities, such as computing, storage, databases, and machine learning. AWS APIs enable developers to build, deploy, and manage applications and services within the AWS ecosystem.

Use cases:

- Developing and deploying scalable web applications using AWS compute, storage, and networking services.
- Building data pipelines and analytics solutions using AWS databases, data warehouses, and big data processing tools.
- Implementing machine learning models and AI-powered services using AWS machine learning platforms and APIs.
- Managing and monitoring AWS resources programmatically, automating tasks, and optimizing infrastructure usage.

Impact: AWS APIs have revolutionized the way developers build and manage applications by providing access to a wide range of cloud-based services and resources. By offering scalable, on-demand infrastructure and platform services, AWS has enabled businesses and developers to create more resilient, flexible, and cost-effective solutions, driving the widespread adoption of cloud computing across various industries.

These real-world API examples demonstrate the power and versatility of APIs in shaping the digital landscape. By providing developers with access to data, services, and resources, APIs have enabled the creation of countless innovative applications and solutions, transforming industries, and empowering businesses to better serve their users and customers. As the world becomes increasingly interconnected and digitized, the role of APIs will continue to grow, offering new opportunities for innovation and collaboration.

6

API Security Basics

API security is a critical aspect of modern software development, as APIs are often responsible for handling sensitive data and connecting various systems and services. Ensuring the security of APIs is essential to protect both the data they manage and the applications that rely on them. In this section, we will explore the basics of API security, focusing on key concepts, best practices, and strategies for keeping APIs safe and secure.

Authentication

Authentication is the process of verifying the identity of a client or user attempting to access an API. Ensuring that only authenticated clients can access an API is a fundamental aspect of API security. There are several authentication methods commonly used in APIs, including:

- API Key: A unique identifier assigned to each client that must be included in API requests. API keys are often used for simple authentication scenarios, as they are easy to implement and manage. However, they may not be suitable for highly sensitive APIs, as they can be easily compromised if not properly protected.
- Basic Authentication: A method that requires clients to provide a username and password with each API request. These credentials are typically Base64-encoded and included in the request header. While simple to implement, Basic Authentication relies on the transmission of credentials in plaintext, making it vulnerable to eavesdropping and interception.
- OAuth: A widely-used standard for delegating access to APIs without sharing user credentials. OAuth enables clients to obtain access tokens, which can be used to authenticate API requests on behalf of users. This approach provides a more secure and flexible authentication mechanism, allowing for granular access control and revocation of permissions.

Authorization

Authorization is the process of determining what actions a client or user is allowed to perform within an API. Implementing proper authorization ensures that clients can only access the resources and perform the actions they are explicitly permitted to, preventing unauthorized access and manipulation of data.

Role-Based Access Control (RBAC) is a common approach to authorization in APIs, where permissions are granted based on predefined roles assigned to users or clients. These roles define the specific actions that can be performed within the API, such as creating, reading, updating, or deleting resources.

Encryption

Encryption is the process of encoding data to protect it from unauthorized access or tampering. Encrypting data transmitted between clients and APIs helps ensure the confidentiality and integrity of sensitive information. There are two primary types of encryption used in API communication:

- Transport Layer Security (TLS): A widely-used protocol for encrypting data transmitted over a network, including API requests and responses. TLS establishes a secure, encrypted channel between the client and the API, preventing eavesdropping, interception, and tampering of data. Implementing TLS for APIs typically involves enabling HTTPS (HTTP over TLS) and acquiring an SSL/TLS certificate for the API domain.
- End-to-end Encryption: A method of encrypting data at the client-side before it is transmitted to the API, ensuring that only the intended recipients can decrypt and access the data. End-to-end encryption is used

in situations where additional layers of protection are required, such as when handling highly sensitive data or complying with strict regulatory requirements.

Input Validation

Input validation is the process of verifying and sanitizing data received from clients to prevent security vulnerabilities, such as injection attacks or cross-site scripting (XSS). By implementing proper input validation, APIs can ensure that only valid and safe data is processed and stored.

API developers should employ a combination of client-side and server-side input validation techniques, including:

- Whitelisting: Defining a set of allowed values or patterns for each input field, and rejecting any inputs that do not meet these criteria.

Blacklisting: Defining a set of disallowed values or patterns for each input field and rejecting any inputs that contain these criteria. However, blacklisting can be less secure than whitelisting, as it requires anticipating and blocking all potential threats.

- Sanitization: Removing or escaping potentially harmful characters or data from user inputs before processing or storing them.
- Length and type checks: Ensuring that inputs meet the

expected length and data type requirements, preventing potential issues related to data processing and storage.

Rate Limiting

Rate limiting is the process of controlling the frequency and volume of API requests from clients to prevent abuse, denial of service (DoS) attacks, and excessive resource consumption. By implementing rate limiting, API developers can protect their systems from being overwhelmed by malicious or misbehaving clients.

API rate limiting can be implemented using various techniques, such as:

- Request quotas: Defining a maximum number of requests that a client can make within a specific time frame (e.g., per minute, hour, or day). Once the quota is reached, the client will be temporarily blocked from making further requests until the time frame resets.
- Throttling: Limiting the rate at which clients can make requests, such as allowing a certain number of requests per second. Throttling can help ensure that API resources are distributed fairly among clients and prevent sudden spikes in traffic from causing performance issues.
- Token bucket algorithms: A more flexible approach to rate limiting that allows clients to accumulate "tokens" over time, which can be spent on making API requests. Token bucket algorithms can help balance the needs of both

high-volume and low-volume clients, providing more equitable access to API resources.

Monitoring and Logging

Monitoring and logging are essential components of API security, enabling developers to detect and respond to potential security incidents or performance issues. By collecting and analyzing logs and metrics from API systems, developers can gain insights into usage patterns, identify potential vulnerabilities, and ensure the overall health and security of their APIs.

API monitoring and logging should include:

- Request and response logging: Capturing details about each API request and response, including timestamps, client information, endpoints, parameters, and status codes. These logs can help developers identify unusual patterns or potential security incidents, such as unauthorized access attempts or high error rates.
- Performance monitoring: Tracking key performance metrics, such as response times, error rates, and resource usage, to ensure that the API is operating efficiently and meeting its service level objectives (SLOs).
- Security monitoring: Implementing tools and processes to detect and alert on potential security threats, such as intrusion detection systems (IDS), security information

and event management (SIEM) solutions, or machine learning-based anomaly detection.

API Security Best Practices

In addition to the fundamental security concepts discussed above, API developers should follow several best practices to ensure the security and integrity of their APIs:

- Keep software and dependencies up-to-date: Regularly update the API's software components and dependencies to address known security vulnerabilities and stay current with industry best practices.
- Implement security headers: Use HTTP security headers, such as Content Security Policy (CSP) and Strict Transport Security (STS), to enhance the security of API communications and protect against various web-based attacks.
- Use secure coding practices: Follow secure coding guidelines and practices, such as the OWASP Top Ten Project, to minimize the risk of introducing security vulnerabilities during development.
- Conduct regular security testing: Perform regular security testing, including penetration testing and vulnerability scanning, to identify and remediate potential security issues in the API.
- Plan for incident response: Develop and maintain an incident response plan to ensure that the API can quickly recover from security incidents and minimize their im-

pact.

By understanding and implementing these API security basics, developers can create more secure, reliable, and resilient APIs, protecting both the data they manage and the applications that rely on them. As APIs continue to play a central role in modern software development and digital transformation, maintaining a strong focus on security will be essential for ensuring the integrity, privacy, and reliability of the interconnected systems and services that underpin today's digital landscape.

1.6.8. Security Compliance and Regulations

APIs that handle sensitive data or operate within regulated industries may be subject to various security compliance requirements and regulations. Ensuring that APIs meet these requirements can help protect sensitive data, minimize legal and financial risks, and maintain the trust of users and customers.

Some of the key security compliance standards and regulations relevant to APIs include:

- General Data Protection Regulation (GDPR): A European Union regulation that governs the handling of personal data and imposes strict requirements on data protection, privacy, and consent. APIs that process personal data of EU residents must comply with GDPR requirements, such as providing transparency about data usage, implementing appropriate security measures, and ensuring data minimization and accuracy.
- Health Insurance Portability and Accountability Act (HIPAA): A United States regulation that sets security and

privacy standards for the handling of protected health information (PHI). APIs that process or store PHI must implement safeguards to protect the confidentiality, integrity, and availability of the data, including access controls, encryption, and auditing.

· Payment Card Industry Data Security Standard (PCI DSS): A set of security standards designed to ensure the safe processing, storage, and transmission of payment card information. APIs that handle payment card data must comply with PCI DSS requirements, such as implementing strong access controls, encryption, and network segmentation.

To maintain compliance with these and other security regulations, API developers should:

· Conduct regular risk assessments: Evaluate the potential risks and vulnerabilities associated with the API's data and operations, and implement appropriate controls to mitigate these risks.

· Implement a security management program: Establish a formal security management program that includes policies, procedures, and guidelines for ensuring the ongoing security and compliance of the API.

· Perform regular audits and assessments: Conduct regular audits and assessments of the API's security controls and compliance status, and address any identified gaps or deficiencies.

By following these API security basics and best practices, developers can ensure the safety and integrity of their APIs, protecting the data they manage and the applications that rely on them. As the digital landscape continues to evolve, maintaining a strong focus on API security will be essential for delivering secure, reliable, and resilient services and solutions.

7

API Versioning

APII versioning is a crucial aspect of API development and management, as it enables developers to introduce changes, updates, and improvements to APIs without disrupting the applications and services that rely on them. In this section, we will explore the importance of API versioning, the different versioning strategies, and best practices for implementing and maintaining versioned APIs.

Why API Versioning is Important

APIs are dynamic by nature, evolving over time as new features are added, bugs are fixed, and underlying technologies change. These updates can potentially break existing clients and integrations if they are not implemented and managed carefully. API versioning allows developers to introduce changes in a controlled and predictable manner, ensuring

that existing clients can continue to function while providing a clear path for adopting new features and improvements.

Some of the key reasons for implementing API versioning include:

- Backward compatibility: Versioning allows developers to maintain backward compatibility with older clients and integrations by preserving the existing functionality and behavior of the API.
- Incremental adoption: Versioning provides a mechanism for clients to adopt new features and improvements at their own pace, minimizing the risk of disruption and ensuring a smooth transition.
- Clear communication: Versioning helps to communicate the changes and updates in the API, making it easier for clients to understand the impact of these changes and plan their adoption accordingly.

API Versioning Strategies

There are several strategies for implementing versioning in APIs, each with its own advantages and trade-offs. Some of the most common API versioning strategies include:

URI Versioning

URI versioning involves including the API version as part of the request's URI, either as a path segment or a query parameter. This approach is simple and easy to implement, as it requires minimal changes to the API's infrastructure and clearly communicates the version being used in the request.
Examples:

- Path segment versioning: **https://api.example.com/v1/users**
- Query parameter versioning: **https://api.example.com/users?version=1**

Pros:

- Easy to implement and understand
- Clearly communicates the version being used

Cons:

- Can result in a proliferation of URIs and endpoints for different versions
- May require significant changes to routing and handling logic as new versions are introduced

Header Versioning

Header versioning involves specifying the API version using a custom HTTP header or the "Accept" header with a custom media type. This approach decouples the version information from the URI, making it easier to manage and evolve the API over time.

Examples:

- Custom header: **X-API-Version: 1**
- Accept header with custom media type: **Accept: application/vnd.example.v1+json**

Pros:

- Decouples version information from the URI
- Supports a more flexible and extensible versioning model

Cons:

- Less visible and intuitive compared to URI versioning
- Requires clients to include additional headers in their requests

Content Negotiation

Content negotiation is a more advanced versioning strategy that relies on the client and server's ability to negotiate the best representation of a resource based on their capabilities and preferences. In this approach, the client specifies its supported versions using the "Accept" header, and the server responds with the most appropriate version based on its own capabilities and the client's preferences.

Example:

- Accept header with version ranges: **Accept: application/json;version=1.0, application/json;version=2.0;q=0.9**

Pros:

- Provides a more flexible and extensible versioning model
- Allows clients and servers to negotiate the best representation of a resource

Cons:

More complex to implement and manage compared to other versioning strategies

- May require additional processing and negotiation logic on both the client and server sides

Choosing the Right Versioning Strategy

Selecting the appropriate versioning strategy for an API depends on various factors, such as the API's requirements, the anticipated frequency of updates, and the preferences of the clients and developers. Some considerations to keep in mind when choosing a versioning strategy include:

- Simplicity and ease of implementation: URI versioning is often the easiest to implement and understand, making it a good choice for smaller APIs or those with less frequent updates.
- Flexibility and extensibility: Header versioning and content negotiation provide a more flexible and extensible versioning model, making them suitable for larger APIs or those with more complex versioning requirements.
- Visibility and communication: URI versioning is the most visible and intuitive, making it easier for clients to understand and adopt new API versions.

API Versioning Best Practices

Implementing and maintaining versioned APIs requires careful planning and management to ensure a smooth transition between versions and minimize the impact on clients and integrations. Some best practices for API versioning include:

Plan for Versioning from the Start

Consider versioning as part of the initial API design process and choose a versioning strategy that aligns with the API's requirements and anticipated updates. Planning for versioning from the beginning can help to avoid potential issues and disruptions as the API evolves.

Use Semantic Versioning

Adopt a semantic versioning scheme, such as the one defined by SemVer (**https://semver.org/**), to clearly communicate the nature and impact of changes in the API. Semantic versioning uses a three-part version number (major.minor.patch) to indicate the type of changes in each release:

- Major: Indicates breaking changes that require clients to modify their code to continue functioning correctly.
- Minor: Indicates backward-compatible changes, such as new features or improvements, that do not require clients to update their code.
- Patch: Indicates backward-compatible bug fixes or se-

curity updates that do not introduce new features or functionality.

Communicate Changes and Updates Clearly

Provide clear documentation and communication about API changes, updates, and versioning policies, including:

- Release notes: Document the changes and updates in each API version, including new features, bug fixes, and breaking changes.
- Migration guides: Provide step-by-step guides and examples for migrating clients and integrations to newer API versions.
- Deprecation notices: Notify clients about upcoming deprecations and removals, giving them sufficient time to update their code and adopt new versions.

Maintain Backward Compatibility

Whenever possible, strive to maintain backward compatibility in API updates to minimize the impact on existing clients and integrations. Avoid making breaking changes unless they are necessary to improve the API's functionality, performance, or security.

Support Multiple Versions

Maintain support for multiple API versions to give clients time to adopt new features and updates at their own pace. Clearly define and communicate the API's versioning policy, including the supported versions and the duration of support for each version.

Test and Validate Versioned APIs

Implement thorough testing and validation processes to ensure the correct functioning of versioned APIs, including:

- Unit and integration testing: Test individual components and their interactions within each API version to ensure they meet their functional requirements.
- Compatibility testing: Test the API's backward compatibility and ensure that older clients and integrations continue to function correctly with newer versions.

Migration testing: Test the migration process and validate that clients can successfully transition from one API version to another without experiencing issues or disruptions.

Deprecating and Sunsetting API Versions

Over time, it may become necessary to deprecate and eventually sunset older API versions to reduce maintenance overhead, improve performance, or address security concerns. It is essential to plan and communicate these deprecations and sunsets carefully to minimize the impact on clients and integrations. Some best practices for deprecating and sunsetting API versions include:

Provide Clear Deprecation Notices

Notify clients well in advance about upcoming deprecations and sunsets, including the affected API versions, the reasons for the deprecation, and the recommended migration paths. Ensure that these notices are clearly communicated through multiple channels, such as API documentation, release notes, developer portals, and direct notifications.

Establish a Deprecation Timeline

Define a clear and reasonable deprecation timeline that provides clients with enough time to update their code and migrate to newer API versions. Consider the complexity of the changes, the potential impact on clients, and the resources required to support multiple versions when determining the deprecation timeline.

Provide Migration Support and Guidance

Assist clients in the migration process by providing comprehensive documentation, migration guides, and support resources. Offer assistance through various channels, such as online forums, email support, and webinars, to help clients address any questions or issues they may encounter during the migration.

Monitor Adoption and Usage Metrics

Track the adoption and usage of different API versions to gauge the impact of deprecations and sunsets on clients and integrations. Use these metrics to inform decisions about extending or adjusting the deprecation timeline and to identify clients who may require additional support or assistance during the migration process.

Retire Deprecated Versions Gracefully

Once the deprecation timeline has elapsed, retire the deprecated API versions in a controlled and predictable manner. Communicate the retirement process and timeline to clients, and consider implementing a phased shutdown that gradually reduces the functionality and performance of the deprecated versions to encourage clients to migrate to newer versions.

In conclusion, API versioning is a critical aspect of API development and management that ensures the seamless evolution of APIs without disrupting the applications and services that rely on them. By understanding the importance of API versioning, adopting the right versioning strategy, and following best practices for implementing and maintaining versioned APIs, developers can successfully navigate the challenges of API updates and provide clients with a stable, reliable, and continuously improving API experience.

II

Designing an API

Designing an API involves creating a well-structured, flexible, and easy-to-use interface that allows clients to interact with a service or application effectively.

8

API Design Principles

D esigning an API is a complex task that requires a deep understanding of the service or application being exposed, as well as the needs and expectations of the clients who will interact with it. To create a successful API, developers should follow a set of guiding principles that promote consistency, simplicity, and ease of use. In this section, we will discuss some fundamental API design principles that can help create a solid foundation for building reliable and effective APIs.

Understand Your Users

An API should be designed with its users in mind. Understand who your target audience is and consider their needs, expectations, and technical capabilities when designing your API. This includes not only the developers who will integrate the API into their applications but also the end-users who will ultimately interact with the service or application through the API.

Provide Clear and Consistent Naming Conventions

Use clear and consistent naming conventions for API resources, endpoints, and parameters. This will make it easier for clients to understand the purpose and function of each API element, reducing the learning curve and ensuring a more intuitive integration experience.

Use Standard HTTP Methods and Status Codes

Leverage standard HTTP methods (GET, POST, PUT, DELETE, etc.) and status codes (200 OK, 201 Created, 400 Bad Request, etc.) to convey the semantics and results of API operations. This not only promotes consistency and predictability but also makes it easier for clients to understand and handle the API's behavior.

Embrace RESTful Design Principles

REST (Representational State Transfer) is a widely adopted architectural style for designing networked APIs that emphasize scalability, simplicity, and statelessness. Embracing RESTful design principles can help create an API that is easy to understand, use, and maintain. Key aspects of RESTful design include:

- Resource-based: Organize the API around resources, which represent the core entities and objects in the application or service.
- Stateless: Ensure that each API request contains all the information needed to process the request, without relying on the server to maintain the state between requests.
- Cacheable: Allow clients to cache responses to improve performance and reduce server load.
- Layered: Separate the API's components into layers, with each layer providing a specific set of functionality.

Support Multiple Formats and Media Types

Design the API to support multiple formats and media types, such as JSON, XML, or CSV, to cater to the diverse needs and preferences of clients. Use content negotiation techniques to allow clients to specify their preferred format and media type, ensuring a more flexible and adaptable API experience.

Provide Extensibility and Backward Compatibility

Design the API with extensibility and backward compatibility in mind, allowing for the introduction of new features and updates without breaking existing clients and integrations. This may involve using versioning strategies, adhering to semantic versioning guidelines, and ensuring that changes to the API are communicated clearly and transparently.

Prioritize Security and Privacy

Ensure that the API is designed with security and privacy as top priorities. Implement appropriate authentication, authorization, and data protection mechanisms to safeguard sensitive information and prevent unauthorized access. Additionally, adhere to relevant data privacy regulations and best practices to protect users' personal information and maintain trust in the API.

Design for Performance and Scalability

Optimize the API's design for performance and scalability, ensuring that it can handle a growing number of clients and requests without compromising the quality of the service. This may involve implementing caching strategies, optimizing database queries, and leveraging asynchronous processing techniques to improve the API's responsiveness and efficiency.

Provide Comprehensive Documentation and Support

Offer comprehensive documentation and support resources to help clients understand and integrate the API effectively. This includes detailed API reference guides, code samples, tutorials, and troubleshooting guides, as well as responsive support channels to address any questions or issues clients may encounter.

Encourage and Facilitate Feedback

Create an open and collaborative environment where clients can provide feedback, report issues, and suggest improvements to the API. This not only helps to identify potential problems and opportunities for enhancement but also fosters a sense of community and engagement among API users.

By adhering to these API design principles, developers can create APIs that are easy to understand, use, and maintain, ensuring a smooth and efficient integration experience for clients. These principles serve as a foundation for building reliable and effective APIs that cater to the diverse needs and expectations of both developers and end-users.

In the following sections, we will delve deeper into specific aspects of API design, such as designing API resources, managing errors, and implementing authentication and authorization mechanisms. These detailed discussions will provide further guidance on how to apply the fundamental design principles outlined in this section to create robust and user-friendly APIs that meet the demands of today's dynamic and interconnected digital landscape.

9

Identifying Use Cases

I dentifying use cases is a critical step in designing an API that meets the needs of its clients. Use cases are scenarios that describe how the API will be used and the functionality it needs to provide to support those use cases. By understanding the use cases for an API, developers can create a design that is tailored to meet the requirements of the clients and optimize the user experience. In this section, we will explore the importance of identifying use cases and discuss strategies for doing so effectively.

Why Identifying Use Cases is Important

Identifying use cases is critical because it helps developers understand the requirements of the API and how it will be used. Use cases allow developers to identify the types of requests that the API will need to handle, the data it will need to provide, and the functionality that it will need to support. This understanding allows developers to design an API that is tailored to meet the specific needs of its clients and optimize the user experience.

Additionally, identifying use cases can help developers identify potential issues and challenges in the API's design. By considering the scenarios in which the API will be used, developers can anticipate and address potential problems that clients may encounter. This proactive approach can help prevent issues from arising in the first place and minimize the impact of any issues that do arise.

Finally, identifying use cases can help developers prioritize their development efforts and allocate resources effectively. By understanding the most critical use cases, developers can focus their efforts on designing and implementing the API's most important features and functionality.

Strategies for Identifying Use Cases

There are several strategies that developers can use to identify use cases for an API. The following are some of the most common and effective approaches:

Analyze User Requirements

One of the most effective strategies for identifying use cases is to analyze the requirements of the API's users. This involves talking to potential clients and end-users to understand their needs, expectations, and pain points. By gathering this information, developers can identify the most critical use cases and design an API that meets those needs.

To conduct user requirement analysis, developers can use various techniques, such as surveys, focus groups, and interviews. These methods allow developers to gather qualitative and quantitative data about user needs and preferences and identify patterns and trends in how the API is likely to be used.

Conduct Competitor Analysis

Another strategy for identifying use cases is to conduct a competitor analysis. This involves analyzing the APIs of competitors or similar services to understand the features and functionality they provide and the use cases they support.

By conducting a competitor analysis, developers can identify gaps and opportunities in the market and gain insights into what clients expect from an API in their industry or niche. This information can inform the design of the API and ensure that it meets the needs of its target audience.

Consider Industry Standards and Best Practices

Developers can also identify use cases by considering industry standards and best practices. This involves analyzing the common use cases and functionality that are expected in a particular industry or niche and incorporating those features into the API's design.

By considering industry standards and best practices, developers can ensure that their API meets the expectations of clients in their industry or niche and provides the functionality they need to be competitive.

Analyze Existing Applications and Services

Developers can also identify use cases by analyzing existing applications and services that are similar to the API they are designing. This involves studying the features and functionality of these applications and services and identifying the use cases that are most common or critical.

By analyzing existing applications and services, developers can gain insights into the types of functionality and features that are most important to clients in their industry or niche. They can also identify opportunities for differentiation and innovation and design an API that provides unique value to its clients.

Conduct User Testing

Finally, developers can identify use cases by conducting user testing. This involves creating prototypes or mockups of the API and testing them with potential clients or end-users. By observing how users interact with the API and gathering feedback, developers can identify the most critical use cases and make adjustments to the API's design to optimize the user experience.

User testing can also help developers identify potential issues or limitations in the API's design and address them before the API is released to clients. This proactive approach can help prevent issues from arising in the first place and minimize the impact of any issues that do arise.

Best Practices for Identifying Use Cases

To identify use cases effectively, developers should follow some best practices, including:

Involve Clients and End-Users

To understand the needs and requirements of the API's clients and end-users, developers should involve them in the process of identifying use cases. This may involve conducting user research, hosting focus groups or workshops, or collaborating with clients to define the API's scope and functionality.

By involving clients and end-users, developers can ensure that the API meets the needs of its target audience and provides a user experience that is optimized for their use cases.

Prioritize Critical Use Cases

Not all use cases are created equal. To prioritize their development efforts and allocate resources effectively, developers should prioritize critical use cases. These are the scenarios that are most essential for the API's success and provide the most significant value to its clients.

By prioritizing critical use cases, developers can ensure that the API meets the most important needs of its clients and provides a user experience that is optimized for those needs.

Iterate and Refine

Identifying use cases is not a one-time process. As the API evolves and the needs of its clients change, developers may need to revisit and refine the use cases they have identified. By iterating and refining the use cases, developers can ensure that the API remains relevant and effective over time.

Consider Future Expansion

When identifying use cases, developers should consider the potential for future expansion and growth. This involves identifying the scenarios that may become critical as the API evolves and designing the API in a way that allows for easy expansion and adaptation.

By considering future expansion, developers can ensure that the API remains relevant and effective over time and provides value to its clients as their needs change and evolve.

In conclusion, identifying use cases is a critical step in designing an API that meets the needs of its clients and optimizes the user experience. By understanding the requirements of its users, considering industry standards and best practices, and conducting user testing, developers can identify the most critical use cases and design an API that provides unique value to its clients. By following best practices, prioritizing critical use cases, and iterating and refining the use cases over time, developers can create an API that remains relevant and effective in today's dynamic and interconnected digital landscape.

10

Defining API Resources

D efining API resources is a critical step in designing an API that is easy to understand and use. API resources are the core components of an API that clients interact with, such as endpoints, data models, and methods. By defining these resources clearly and consistently, developers can create an API that is intuitive and easy to use, reducing the learning curve for clients and increasing adoption rates. In this section, we will explore the importance of defining API resources and discuss strategies for doing so effectively.

Why Defining API Resources is Important

Defining API resources is important because it helps to create a clear and consistent API design that is easy to understand and use. By defining API resources clearly and consistently, developers can ensure that clients understand how to interact with the API and what data and functionality it provides.

Clear and consistent API resources also reduce the learning curve for clients, making it easier for them to integrate the API into their applications and services. This can increase adoption rates and help to build a strong user base for the API.

Finally, well-defined API resources facilitate maintenance and updates to the API over time. By establishing a consistent design and documentation for API resources, developers can make changes to the API more easily and avoid breaking changes that may disrupt clients' applications or services.

Strategies for Defining API Resources

There are several strategies that developers can use to define API resources effectively. The following are some of the most common and effective approaches:

Use Standard HTTP Methods and Status Codes

One of the most effective strategies for defining API resources is to use standard HTTP methods and status codes. This involves using standard HTTP methods, such as GET, POST, PUT, and DELETE, to define the functionality and operations of the API's resources. It also involves using standard HTTP status codes, such as 200 OK and 404 Not Found, to provide feedback to clients about the status of their requests.

By using standard HTTP methods and status codes, developers can create an API that is intuitive and easy to use, reducing the learning curve for clients and increasing adoption rates. Additionally, using standard HTTP methods and status codes facilitates interoperability with other APIs and services that use the same standards.

Use Consistent Naming Conventions

Another strategy for defining API resources is to use consistent naming conventions. This involves defining a consistent naming convention for endpoints, data models, and methods that are used throughout the API. By using consistent naming conventions, developers can create an API that is easy to understand and use, reducing confusion and increasing adoption rates.

Consistent naming conventions also facilitate maintenance and updates to the API over time. By establishing a consistent naming convention, developers can make changes to the API more easily and avoid breaking changes that may disrupt clients' applications or services.

Use HATEOAS

Hypermedia as the Engine of Application State (HATEOAS) is a RESTful design principle that involves using hyperlinks to represent relationships between resources in an API. By using hyperlinks, developers can create a self-describing API that is easy to navigate and understand.

Using HATEOAS facilitates client discovery and interaction with API resources, reducing the learning curve and increasing adoption rates. Additionally, using HATEOAS can make the API more flexible and adaptable to changes over time.

Use Data Models

Using data models is another strategy for defining API resources. Data models define the structure and format of the data that is exchanged between the API and its clients. By using data models, developers can ensure that the API's resources are well-structured and easy to understand.

Data models also facilitate data validation and error handling, making it easier to identify and resolve issues with data exchange between the API and its clients.

To use data models effectively, developers should use a consistent and clear format, such as JSON or XML, and ensure that the data models are well-documented and easy to understand. This will make it easier for clients to interact with the API's resources and reduce the likelihood of errors or misunderstandings.

Best Practices for Defining API Resources

To define API resources effectively, developers should follow some best practices, including:

Use Clear and Consistent Naming Conventions

Using clear and consistent naming conventions is essential for defining API resources effectively. Developers should establish a naming convention that is easy to understand and use and apply it consistently throughout the API. This will make it easier for clients to understand how to interact with the API's resources and reduce confusion and errors.

Use Standard HTTP Methods and Status Codes

Using standard HTTP methods and status codes is also important for defining API resources effectively. Developers should use the standard HTTP methods, such as GET, POST, PUT, and DELETE, to define the functionality and operations of the API's resources. They should also use standard HTTP status codes, such as 200 OK and 404 Not Found, to provide feedback to clients about the status of their requests.

By using standard HTTP methods and status codes, developers can create an API that is intuitive and easy to use, reducing the learning curve for clients and increasing adoption rates.

Use Data Models Effectively

Using data models effectively is also critical for defining API resources. Developers should use well-structured and well-documented data models to define the structure and format of the data that is exchanged between the API and its clients. This will ensure that the API's resources are well-defined and easy to understand and facilitate data validation and error handling.

Use HATEOAS

Using HATEOAS is another best practice for defining API resources effectively. Developers should use hyperlinks to represent relationships between resources in the API, creating a self-describing API that is easy to navigate and understand. This will facilitate client discovery and interaction with API resources, reducing the learning curve and increasing adoption rates.

In conclusion, defining API resources is a critical step in designing an API that is easy to understand and use. By using standard HTTP methods and status codes, consistent naming conventions, data models, and HATEOAS, developers can create an API that is well-defined and easy to navigate. By following best practices, developers can create an API that is intuitive, easy to use, and well-documented, reducing the learning curve for clients and increasing adoption rates.

11

Designing API Endpoints

D esigning API endpoints is a critical step in creating an API that is easy to use and understand. API endpoints are the entry points to an API that clients interact with, allowing them to access the API's resources and functionality. In this section, we will explore the importance of designing API endpoints and discuss strategies for doing so effectively.

Why Designing API Endpoints is Important

Designing API endpoints is important because it defines how clients interact with the API and access its resources and functionality. By designing API endpoints effectively, developers can create an API that is intuitive and easy to use, reducing the learning curve for clients and increasing adoption rates.

Effective API endpoint design also facilitates maintenance and updates to the API over time. By establishing a consistent design for API endpoints, developers can make changes to the API more easily and avoid breaking changes that may disrupt clients' applications or services.

Strategies for Designing API Endpoints

There are several strategies that developers can use to design API endpoints effectively. The following are some of the most common and effective approaches:

Use Simple and Intuitive URL Structures

One of the most effective strategies for designing API endpoints is to use simple and intuitive URL structures. This involves defining URL structures that are easy to understand and use, reducing the learning curve for clients and increasing adoption rates.

Simple and intuitive URL structures also facilitate maintenance and updates to the API over time. By using a consistent URL structure, developers can make changes to the API more easily and avoid breaking changes that may disrupt clients' applications or services.

Use Resource-Oriented Design

Resource-oriented design is a design approach that focuses on defining API endpoints around the resources that clients interact with. This involves defining endpoints that represent the resources that clients need to access and the operations that they can perform on those resources.

By using resource-oriented design, developers can create an API that is intuitive and easy to use, reducing the learning curve for clients and increasing adoption rates. Resource-oriented design also facilitates maintenance and updates to the API over time, making it easier to make changes without disrupting clients' applications or services.

Use HTTP Verbs Effectively

HTTP verbs are the methods that clients use to interact with API endpoints, such as GET, POST, PUT, and DELETE. Effective use of HTTP verbs can make API endpoints more intuitive and easy to use.

Developers should use HTTP verbs effectively, defining their use consistently across the API. This will make it easier for clients to understand how to interact with the API's resources and reduce confusion and errors.

Use Query Parameters Effectively

Query parameters are a way for clients to filter and search for specific data within an API's resources. Effective use of query parameters can make API endpoints more flexible and adaptable to clients' needs.

Developers should use query parameters effectively, defining their use consistently across the API. This will make it easier for clients to understand how to filter and search for data within the API's resources and reduce confusion and errors.

Best Practices for Designing API Endpoints

To design API endpoints effectively, developers should follow some best practices, including:

Use Clear and Consistent URL Structures

Using clear and consistent URL structures is essential for designing API endpoints effectively. Developers should establish a URL structure that is easy to understand and use and apply it consistently throughout the API. This will make it easier for clients to understand how to interact with the API's resources and reduce confusion and errors.

Use Resource-Oriented Design

Using resource-oriented design is another best practice for designing API endpoints effectively. Developers should define API endpoints around the resources that clients interact with, making it easier for clients to understand how to access and use the API's resources. Resource-oriented design also facilitates maintenance and updates to the API over time, making it easier to make changes without disrupting clients' applications or services.

Use HTTP Verbs Effectively

Using HTTP verbs effectively is also critical for designing API endpoints. Developers should use HTTP verbs consistently across the API, defining their use clearly and effectively. This will make it easier for clients to understand how to interact with the API's resources and reduce confusion and errors.

Use Query Parameters Effectively

Using query parameters effectively is another best practice for designing API endpoints. Developers should define the use of query parameters consistently across the API, making it easier for clients to filter and search for data within the API's resources. This will make the API more flexible and adaptable to clients' needs and reduce confusion and errors.

Examples of API Endpoint Design

To illustrate effective API endpoint design, let's look at some examples from popular APIs:

Twitter API

The Twitter API uses a resource-oriented design, defining endpoints around resources such as tweets, users, and time-lines. For example, to retrieve a user's tweets, the following endpoint can be used:

```
GET /1.1/statuses/user_timeline.json?
screen_name={screen_name}&count={count}
```

This endpoint uses the GET HTTP verb to retrieve data and includes query parameters to filter the results by screen name and count. The endpoint is well-structured and easy to understand, making it easy for clients to interact with the API's resources.

Stripe API

The Stripe API uses a resource-oriented design as well, defining endpoints around resources such as charges, customers, and subscriptions. For example, to create a charge, the following endpoint can be used:

```
POST /v1/charges
```

This endpoint uses the POST HTTP verb to create a new resource and includes a well-defined data model that specifies the required and optional fields for creating a charge. The endpoint is simple and intuitive, making it easy for clients to use and reducing the learning curve.

Google Maps API

The Google Maps API uses a resource-oriented design to define endpoints around resources such as maps, geocoding, and directions. For example, to retrieve a route between two points, the following endpoint can be used:

```
GET /maps/api/directions/json?
origin={origin}&destination={destination}
```

This endpoint uses the GET HTTP verb to retrieve data and includes query parameters to define the origin and destination of the route. The endpoint is well-structured and easy to use, making it easy for clients to access the API's resources.

In conclusion, designing API endpoints is a critical step in creating an API that is easy to use and understand. By using simple and intuitive URL structures, resource-oriented design, effective use of HTTP verbs and query parameters, developers can create an API that is intuitive and easy to use, reducing the learning curve for clients and increasing adoption rates. By following best practices and using examples from popular APIs, developers can design API endpoints effectively and create an API that is well-documented and easy to maintain over time.

12

Choosing the Right Data Format

C hoosing the right data format is an essential part of designing an API that is easy to use and understand. The data format defines how data is exchanged between the API and its clients and can have a significant impact on the API's performance, flexibility, and ease of use. In this section, we will explore the importance of choosing the right data format and discuss some of the most common data formats used in modern APIs.

Why Choosing the Right Data Format is Important

Choosing the right data format is important because it defines how data is exchanged between the API and its clients. The data format can have a significant impact on the API's performance, flexibility, and ease of use.

An effective data format can make it easier for clients to

understand and interact with the API's resources, reducing the learning curve and increasing adoption rates. It can also facilitate maintenance and updates to the API over time, making it easier to make changes without disrupting clients' applications or services.

Common Data Formats Used in APIs

There are several common data formats used in modern APIs. The following are some of the most popular and effective data formats:

JSON

JSON (JavaScript Object Notation) is a lightweight and flexible data format that is widely used in modern APIs. JSON is based on a simple and intuitive syntax that makes it easy to read and write, even for developers who are new to API development.

JSON is also well-supported by most programming languages and frameworks, making it easy to integrate into existing applications and services. Additionally, JSON is highly interoperable, meaning that it can be used across different platforms and systems without the need for extensive conversion or translation.

XML

XML (Extensible Markup Language) is another widely used data format in modern APIs. XML is a versatile and powerful data format that supports a wide range of data types and structures.

XML is well-supported by most programming languages and frameworks, making it easy to integrate into existing applications and services. Additionally, XML is highly extensible, meaning that it can be customized to support specific data structures and types.

CSV

CSV (Comma-Separated Values) is a simple and efficient data format that is often used for exchanging tabular data between systems. CSV is based on a simple and intuitive syntax that makes it easy to read and write, even for developers who are new to API development.

CSV is also highly interoperable, meaning that it can be used across different platforms and systems without the need for extensive conversion or translation. Additionally, CSV is highly efficient, meaning that it can be used to exchange large amounts of data quickly and easily.

YAML

YAML (Yet Another Markup Language) is a data format that is designed to be human-readable and easy to write. YAML is based on a simple and intuitive syntax that makes it easy to understand and use.

YAML is well-supported by most programming languages and frameworks, making it easy to integrate into existing applications and services. Additionally, YAML is highly extensible, meaning that it can be customized to support specific data structures and types.

Best Practices for Choosing a Data Format

To choose a data format effectively, developers should follow some best practices, including:

Use a Consistent Data Format

Using a consistent data format is essential for designing an API that is easy to use and understand. Developers should choose a data format that is well-supported by most programming languages and frameworks and use it consistently throughout the API.

This will make it easier for clients to understand how to interact with the API's resources and reduce confusion and errors.

Choose a Data Format Based on the Use Case

Choosing a data format based on the use case is also important for designing an API that is effective and efficient. Different data formats have different strengths and weaknesses, and developers should choose a data format that is appropriate for the specific use case.

For example, JSON is a good choice for APIs that exchange complex data structures, while CSV is better suited for APIs that exchange tabular data. Developers should consider the type of data being exchanged and the needs of the clients when choosing a data format.

Document the Data Format

Documenting the data format is essential for designing an API that is well-documented and easy to use. Developers should provide clear and concise documentation for the data format, including examples and best practices for using it effectively.

This will make it easier for clients to understand how to interact with the API's resources and reduce confusion and errors.

Examples of API Data Formats

To illustrate effective API data format design, let's look at some examples from popular APIs:

GitHub API

The GitHub API uses JSON as its primary data format for exchanging data between the API and its clients. JSON is a good choice for the GitHub API because it supports complex data structures and is well-supported by most programming languages and frameworks.

The GitHub API also provides clear and concise documentation for the JSON data format, including examples and best practices for using it effectively.

Stripe API

The Stripe API uses JSON as its primary data format for exchanging data between the API and its clients. JSON is a good choice for the Stripe API because it supports complex data structures and is well-supported by most programming languages and frameworks.

The Stripe API also provides clear and concise documentation for the JSON data format, including examples and best practices for using it effectively.

OpenWeatherMap API

The OpenWeatherMap API uses both JSON and XML as data formats for exchanging data between the API and its clients. XML is a good choice for the OpenWeatherMap API because it supports a wide range of data types and structures, while JSON is a good choice for its lightweight and flexible syntax.

The OpenWeatherMap API also provides clear and concise documentation for both the XML and JSON data formats, including examples and best practices for using them effectively.

In conclusion, choosing the right data format is essential for designing an API that is easy to use and understand. By choosing a data format based on the use case, using a consistent data format, and documenting the data format effectively, developers can create an API that is well-documented, efficient, and effective. By using examples from popular APIs, developers can design API data formats effectively and create an API that is well-supported and easy to maintain over time.

13

Status Codes and Error Handling

S tatus codes and error handling are essential components of any API. They enable the API to communicate
effectively with clients, informing them of the success
or failure of their requests and providing useful information
to help troubleshoot and debug errors.

In this section, we will explore the importance of status
codes and error handling in API design, discuss the most
common status codes and error handling strategies, and
provide examples of effective status code and error handling
design.

Importance of Status Codes and Error Handling in API Design

Status codes and error handling are critical components of API design because they enable the API to communicate effectively with clients. By providing clear and concise feedback on the success or failure of clients' requests, status codes and error handling help reduce confusion and errors, improve performance, and enhance the user experience.

Effective status codes and error handling also facilitate maintenance and updates to the API over time, making it easier to make changes without disrupting clients' applications or services. By providing clear and concise information about errors and failures, developers can quickly identify and resolve issues, reducing downtime and improving reliability.

Common Status Codes

HTTP status codes are the most common status codes used in API design. HTTP status codes are standardized codes that are used by servers to indicate the success or failure of a client's request.

The following are some of the most common HTTP status codes used in API design:

200 OK

The 200 OK status code indicates that the client's request was successful, and the server has returned the requested data. This status code is typically used for GET and PUT requests.

201 Created

The 201 Created status code indicates that the server has successfully created a new resource in response to the client's request. This status code is typically used for POST requests.

204 No Content

The 204 No Content status code indicates that the server has successfully processed the client's request, but there is no data to return. This status code is typically used for DELETE requests.

400 Bad Request

The 400 Bad Request status code indicates that the client's request was malformed or invalid. This status code is typically used when the client has provided incorrect or incomplete data.

401 Unauthorized

The 401 Unauthorized status code indicates that the client's request could not be authenticated. This status code is typically used when the client has provided incorrect or invalid credentials.

403 Forbidden

The 403 Forbidden status code indicates that the client's request was valid, but the server is refusing to fulfill it. This status code is typically used when the client does not have sufficient permissions to access the requested resource.

404 Not Found

The 404 Not Found status code indicates that the server could not find the requested resource. This status code is typically used when the client has requested a resource that does not exist.

500 Internal Server Error

The 500 Internal Server Error status code indicates that an unexpected error has occurred on the server. This status code is typically used when the server is unable to fulfill the client's request due to a system or application error.

Error Handling Strategies

Effective error handling is critical for API design. Error handling strategies should be designed to provide clear and concise feedback on the success or failure of clients' requests and to provide useful information to help troubleshoot and debug errors.

The following are some of the most common error handling strategies used in API design:

Use Descriptive Error Messages

Descriptive error messages are essential for effective error handling in API design. Error messages should provide clear and concise information about the nature of the error and how to resolve it.

Descriptive error messages can help reduce confusion and errors, improve performance, and enhance the user experience. By providing clear and concise information about errors and failures, developers can quickly identify and resolve issues, reducing downtime and improving reliability.

Use Standardized Error Messages

Using standardized error messages can help improve the consistency and reliability of error handling in API design. Standardized error messages enable developers to use consistent language and terminology, reducing confusion and errors.

Standardized error messages can also make it easier for developers to troubleshoot and debug errors, as they can quickly identify and resolve common issues.

Provide Useful Information in Error Responses

Error responses should provide useful information to help clients troubleshoot and debug errors. Error responses should include the HTTP status code, a descriptive error message, and any additional information that may be helpful, such as a timestamp, stack trace, or request ID.

Providing useful information in error responses can help reduce confusion and errors, improve performance, and enhance the user experience.

Use Rate Limiting to Manage API Usage

Rate limiting is a strategy that can be used to manage API usage and prevent abuse. Rate limiting involves restricting the number of requests that a client can make within a specific time frame.

By using rate limiting, developers can prevent clients from overwhelming the API with requests, ensuring that the API remains stable and reliable.

Use Retry Mechanisms to Handle Temporary Errors

Retry mechanisms can be used to handle temporary errors that occur when the API is experiencing high traffic or when there is a network issue. Retry mechanisms involve retrying the request after a certain period of time has elapsed.

By using retry mechanisms, developers can reduce the likelihood of errors and improve the reliability of the API.

Examples of Effective Status Code and Error Handling Design

To illustrate effective status code and error handling design, let's look at some examples from popular APIs:

Twilio API

The Twilio API uses HTTP status codes to communicate the success or failure of clients' requests. Twilio also provides descriptive error messages and additional information to help clients troubleshoot and debug errors.

For example, if a client attempts to send an SMS message to a phone number that is not valid, Twilio returns a 400 Bad Request status code and a descriptive error message indicating the reason for the failure.

Stripe API

The Stripe API uses HTTP status codes to communicate the success or failure of clients' requests. Stripe also provides descriptive error messages and additional information to help clients troubleshoot and debug errors.

For example, if a client attempts to create a new payment method with invalid payment details, Stripe returns a 400 Bad Request status code and a descriptive error message indicating the reason for the failure.

GitHub API

The GitHub API uses HTTP status codes to communicate the success or failure of clients' requests. GitHub also provides descriptive error messages and additional information to help clients troubleshoot and debug errors.

For example, if a client attempts to create a new repository with a name that is already in use, GitHub returns a 422 Unprocessable Entity status code and a descriptive error message indicating the reason for the failure.

In conclusion, status codes and error handling are essential components of API design. By providing clear and concise feedback on the success or failure of clients' requests and providing useful information to help troubleshoot and debug errors, developers can create an API that is reliable, efficient, and effective. Common HTTP status codes are used to communicate the success or failure of requests, while error handling strategies should provide clear and concise feedback on the nature of the error and how to resolve it.

Effective error handling should use descriptive and standardized error messages, provide useful information in error responses, and use rate limiting and retry mechanisms to manage API usage and handle temporary errors. By using examples from popular APIs, developers can design effective status code and error handling systems and create APIs that are well-supported and easy to maintain over time.

Best Practices for Status Codes and Error Handling in API Design

In addition to the strategies discussed above, there are several best practices that developers should follow when designing status codes and error handling systems in API design:

Use HTTP Status Codes Appropriately

HTTP status codes should be used appropriately to communicate the success or failure of clients' requests. Using status codes inconsistently or inappropriately can lead to confusion and errors.

Provide Clear and Concise Error Messages

Error messages should be clear and concise, providing useful information to help clients troubleshoot and debug errors. Vague or ambiguous error messages can lead to confusion and errors.

Use Consistent Terminology and Language

Consistent terminology and language should be used throughout the API to reduce confusion and errors. Using inconsistent terminology or language can make it difficult for clients to understand how to interact with the API.

Document the Status Code and Error Handling System

The status code and error handling system should be well-documented, providing clear and concise information on how to interpret status codes and error messages. Clear documentation can reduce confusion and errors and make it easier for clients to interact with the API.

Test the Status Code and Error Handling System

The status code and error handling system should be thoroughly tested to ensure that it is working as intended. Testing can help identify issues and improve the reliability of the API.

Continuously Monitor and Improve the Status Code and Error Handling System

The status code and error handling system should be continuously monitored and improved to ensure that it is effective and efficient. By monitoring the system and making improvements over time, developers can create an API that is reliable and easy to use.

In conclusion, effective status code and error handling design is critical for API design. By using common HTTP status codes, providing descriptive error messages, and using standardized terminology and language, developers can create an API that is easy to use and understand. By following best practices and continuously monitoring and improving the status code and error handling system, developers can create an API that is reliable, efficient, and effective.

14

API Documentation

API documentation is an essential component of API design, providing developers with the information they need to interact with the API effectively. Effective API documentation should be clear, concise, and comprehensive, providing developers with the information they need to understand how to use the API, its resources, and its endpoints.

In this section, we will explore the importance of API documentation in API design, discuss the elements of effective API documentation, and provide examples of effective API documentation.

Importance of API Documentation in API Design

API documentation is critical for API design because it provides developers with the information they need to interact with the API effectively. API documentation should be clear, concise, and comprehensive, providing developers with the information they need to understand how to use the API, its resources, and its endpoints.

Effective API documentation can help reduce confusion and errors, improve performance, and enhance the user experience. By providing clear and concise information about the API's resources and endpoints, developers can quickly identify and resolve issues, reducing downtime and improving reliability.

Elements of Effective API Documentation

Effective API documentation should contain the following elements:

Overview

The overview should provide a brief introduction to the API, including its purpose, functionality, and any key features or benefits. The overview should provide a high-level view of the API, providing developers with a clear understanding of what the API does and how it can be used.

Getting Started

The getting started section should provide developers with the information they need to begin using the API, including instructions on how to obtain API credentials, how to authenticate requests, and how to use the API's resources and endpoints.

Resources and Endpoints

The resources and endpoints section should provide a detailed description of each of the API's resources and endpoints. Each resource and endpoint should be described in detail, including its purpose, functionality, and any required parameters or data formats.

Authentication

The authentication section should describe the authentication mechanisms used by the API, including any required credentials or tokens. The authentication section should provide clear instructions on how to authenticate requests to the API, including any relevant code examples.

Rate Limiting and Throttling

The rate limiting and throttling section should describe the rate limiting and throttling mechanisms used by the API, including any restrictions on the number of requests that can be made within a specific time frame.

Error Handling

The error handling section should describe the error handling mechanisms used by the API, including the HTTP status codes used to communicate the success or failure of clients' requests, and any additional error information that may be provided.

Examples

The examples section should provide developers with code examples of how to use the API's resources and endpoints. Code examples should be clear and concise, demonstrating how to perform common tasks and functions using the API.

API Reference

The API reference should provide a complete and comprehensive list of all the API's resources and endpoints, including any required parameters or data formats. The API reference should be well-organized and easy to navigate, providing developers with quick and easy access to the information they need.

Examples of Effective API Documentation

To illustrate effective API documentation, let's look at some examples from popular APIs:

Stripe API

The Stripe API documentation is clear, concise, and comprehensive, providing developers with all the information they need to interact with the API effectively. The Stripe API documentation includes an overview of the API, a getting started guide, detailed descriptions of resources and endpoints, authentication mechanisms, rate limiting and throttling information, error handling mechanisms, code examples, and an API reference.

The Stripe API documentation is well-organized and easy to navigate, providing developers with quick and easy access to the information they need. The documentation includes detailed descriptions of each endpoint, including examples of how to use the endpoint and any required parameters or data formats.

GitHub API

The GitHub API documentation is another excellent example of effective API documentation. The documentation includes an overview of the API, a getting started guide, detailed descriptions of resources and endpoints, authentication mechanisms, rate limiting and throttling information, error handling mechanisms, code examples, and an API reference.

The GitHub API documentation is well-organized and easy to navigate, providing developers with quick and easy access to the information they need. The documentation includes detailed descriptions of each endpoint, including examples of how to use the endpoint and any required parameters or data formats.

Twilio API

The Twilio API documentation is also an excellent example of effective API documentation. The documentation includes an overview of the API, a getting started guide, detailed descriptions of resources and endpoints, authentication mechanisms, rate limiting and throttling information, error handling mechanisms, code examples, and an API reference.

The Twilio API documentation is well-organized and easy to navigate, providing developers with quick and easy access to the information they need. The documentation includes detailed descriptions of each endpoint, including examples of how to use the endpoint and any required parameters or data formats.

In conclusion, API documentation is an essential component of API design. Effective API documentation should be clear, concise, and comprehensive, providing developers with the information they need to interact with the API effectively. By including an overview, getting started guide, detailed descriptions of resources and endpoints, authentication mechanisms, rate limiting and throttling information, error handling mechanisms, code examples, and an API reference, developers can create effective API documentation that is well-supported and easy to maintain over time.

III

Building a RESTful API

REST (Representational State Transfer) is a popular architectural style for building web services and APIs. In this chapter, we will explore the principles of REST architecture, discuss the benefits of using REST in API design, and provide a step-by-step guide for building a RESTful API.

15

REST Architecture Principles

R EST is based on a set of architectural principles that emphasize scalability, reliability, and simplicity. The following are the key principles of REST architecture:

Client-Server Architecture

The client-server architecture is a fundamental principle of REST, where the client and server are separated from each other. The client sends requests to the server, which processes the request and sends a response back to the client. This separation of concerns allows for the client and server to evolve independently, improving scalability and performance.

Statelessness

In REST architecture, each request from the client to the server is independent and self-contained. The server does not store any client context between requests, which makes the API stateless. This simplifies the architecture and improves scalability, as the server can handle multiple requests simultaneously without the need to manage client context.

Cacheability

REST architecture allows for responses to be cached by the client or any intermediate server, such as a proxy server. This improves performance by reducing the number of requests sent to the server and minimizing the time spent waiting for a response.

Layered System

REST architecture allows for a layered system, where the client may interact with a server through an intermediary, such as a load balancer or proxy server. This improves scalability and reliability, as each layer can perform its own function independently and can be added or removed without affecting the overall system.

Uniform Interface

The uniform interface is a key principle of REST architecture, defining a set of constraints that must be followed by both the client and server to communicate effectively. The uniform interface includes the following four constraints:

- Resource identification: Resources are identified using a unique URI (Uniform Resource Identifier), which allows for the identification and manipulation of resources.
- Resource manipulation through representations: Resources are manipulated through representations, such as JSON or XML, which provide a standardized way of exchanging information between the client and server.
- Self-descriptive messages: Each message sent from the client to the server and vice versa should contain enough information to describe how the message should be processed.
- Hypermedia as the engine of application state (HATEOAS): The server should provide links to related resources in each response, allowing clients to navigate the API and discover available resources.

By following the uniform interface constraint, developers can create APIs that are scalable, reliable, and easy to use.

Benefits of Using REST in API Design

REST architecture provides several benefits for API design, including:

- Scalability: REST architecture allows for the separation of concerns between the client and server, which improves scalability.
- Performance: REST architecture allows for responses to be cached, reducing the number of requests sent to the server and minimizing the time spent waiting for a response.
- Flexibility: REST architecture allows for a layered system, which can be added or removed without affecting the overall system.
- Ease of Use: REST architecture provides a uniform interface, making it easy for developers to understand and interact with the API.

In conclusion, REST architecture is a popular and effective architectural style for building web services and APIs. By following the principles of REST architecture, developers can create APIs that are scalable, reliable, and easy to use.

16

Implementing CRUD Operations

C RUD (Create, Read, Update, Delete) operations are the basic operations that an API should support to enable data manipulation. In this section, we will explore how to implement CRUD operations in a RESTful API, including creating resources, retrieving resources, updating resources, and deleting resources.

Creating Resources

To create a resource in a RESTful API, a client sends a POST request to the server with the resource's representation in the request body. The server then creates the resource and returns a response with the URI of the newly created resource in the Location header.

For example, to create a new user resource in a users resource collection, a client might send a POST request to the following URI:

```
POST /users
```

The request body might contain the following representation of the new user:

```
{
  "name": "John Doe",
  "email": "johndoe@example.com",
  "age": 30
}
```

The server would then create the new user and return a response with the URI of the new user in the Location header:

```
HTTP/1.1 201 Created
Location: /users/12345
```

Retrieving Resources

To retrieve a resource in a RESTful API, a client sends a GET request to the server with the URI of the resource. The server then returns a response with the representation of the resource in the response body.

For example, to retrieve the user with the ID 12345, a client might send a GET request to the following URI:

```
GET /users/12345
```

The server would then return a response with the representation of the user in the response body:

```
HTTP/1.1 200 OK
Content-Type: application/json

{
  "id": "12345",
  "name": "John Doe",
  "email": "johndoe@example.com",
  "age": 30
}
```

Updating Resources

To update a resource in a RESTful API, a client sends a PUT or PATCH request to the server with the URI of the resource and the updated representation of the resource in the request body. The server then updates the resource and returns a response with the updated representation of the resource in the response body.

For example, to update the user with the ID 12345, a client might send a PUT or PATCH request to the following URI:

```
PUT /users/12345
```

or

```
PATCH /users/12345
```

The request body might contain the updated representation of the user:

```
{
  "name": "Jane Doe",
  "email": "janedoe@example.com",
  "age": 35
}
```

The server would then update the user and return a response with the updated representation of the user in the response body:

```
HTTP/1.1 200 OK
Content-Type: application/json

{
  "id": "12345",
  "name": "Jane Doe",
  "email": "janedoe@example.com",
  "age": 35
}
```

Deleting Resources

To delete a resource in a RESTful API, a client sends a DELETE request to the server with the URI of the resource. The server then deletes the resource and returns a response with a status code of 204 (No Content).

For example, to delete the user with the ID 12345, a client might send a DELETE request to the following URI:

```
DELETE /users/12345
```

The server would then delete the user and return a response with a status code of 204 (No Content):

```
HTTP/1.1 204 No Content
```

Best Practices for Implementing CRUD Operations

When implementing CRUD operations in a RESTful API, it is important to follow best practices to ensure that the API is efficient, maintainable, and secure. The following are some best practices for implementing CRUD operations:

- Use HTTP methods correctly: Use the appropriate HTTP method for each operation (POST for creating resources, GET for retrieving resources, PUT or PATCH for updating resources, and DELETE for deleting resources).

- Use HTTP status codes correctly: Use the appropriate HTTP status code to indicate the success or failure of each operation.
- Use resource URIs correctly: Use unique URIs to identify resources and follow a consistent URI pattern for all resources.
- Use consistent data formats: Use a consistent data format, such as JSON or XML, for all resource representations.
- Implement input validation: Validate input data to prevent errors and security vulnerabilities.
- Implement authentication and authorization: Implement authentication and authorization mechanisms to protect sensitive data and operations.
- Implement rate limiting and throttling: Implement rate limiting and throttling mechanisms to prevent abuse and ensure fair usage of the API.

By following these best practices, developers can create RESTful APIs that are efficient, maintainable, and secure.

In conclusion, implementing CRUD operations is a fundamental aspect of building a RESTful API. By following best practices for creating, retrieving, updating, and deleting resources, developers can create APIs that are efficient, maintainable, and secure.

17

Handling Relationships between Resources

In a RESTful API, resources can be related to each other in various ways. For example, a blog post resource may have related comments, or a customer resource may have related orders. In this section, we will explore how to handle relationships between resources in a RESTful API, including one-to-one, one-to-many, and many-to-many relationships.

One-to-One Relationships

In a one-to-one relationship, a resource is related to another resource in a one-to-one manner. For example, a user resource may have a profile resource that contains additional information about the user.

To handle one-to-one relationships in a RESTful API, the

resource that has the relationship should contain a reference to the related resource. For example, the user resource may contain a link to the profile resource:

```
GET /users/12345

{
  "id": "12345",
  "name": "John Doe",
  "email": "johndoe@example.com",
  "profile": {
    "href": "/profiles/67890"
  }
}
```

The client can then follow the link to retrieve the related resource:

```
GET /profiles/67890

{
  "id": "67890",
  "bio": "I am a software developer.",
  "website": "https://example.com"
}
```

One-to-Many Relationships

In a one-to-many relationship, a resource is related to multiple instances of another resource. For example, a blog post resource may have multiple comments.

To handle one-to-many relationships in a RESTful API, the resource that has the relationship should contain a list of links to the related resources. For example, the blog post resource may contain links to the related comment resources:

```
GET /posts/12345

{
  "id": "12345",
  "title": "My First Blog Post",
  "content": "This is my first blog post.",
  "comments": [
    {
      "href": "/comments/67890"
    },
    {
      "href": "/comments/12345"
    }
  ]
}
```

The client can then follow the links to retrieve the related resources:

```
GET /comments/67890

{
  "id": "67890",
  "author": "Jane Doe",
  "content": "Great post!",
  "created_at": "2022-01-01T00:00:00Z"
```

```
}

GET /comments/12345

{
  "id": "12345",
  "author": "Bob Smith",
  "content": "Thanks for sharing!",
  "created_at": "2022-01-02T00:00:00Z"
}
```

Many-to-Many Relationships

In a many-to-many relationship, a resource is related to multiple instances of another resource, and vice versa. For example, a user may have multiple roles, and a role may be assigned to multiple users.

To handle many-to-many relationships in a RESTful API, a third resource should be created to represent the relationship between the two resources. For example, a user role resource may be created to represent the relationship between a user and a role:

```
GET /users/12345

{
  "id": "12345",
  "name": "John Doe",
```

```
  "email": "johndoe@example.com",
  "roles": [
    {
      "href": "/user_roles/1"
    },
    {
      "href": "/user_roles/2"
    }
  ]
}
GET /roles/1

{
  "id": "1",
  "name": "Admin",
  "description": "Admin role"
}


GET /user_roles/1

{
  "id": "1",
  "user": {
    "href": "/users/12345"
  },
  "role": {
    "href": "/roles/1"
  }
}
```

By creating a separate resource to represent the relationship
between the user and the role, we can handle many-to-many
relationships in a RESTful API in a structured and efficient
manner.

Best Practices for Handling Relationships

When handling relationships between resources in a RESTful API, it is important to follow best practices to ensure that the API is efficient, maintainable, and scalable. The following are some best practices for handling relationships:

- Use resource URIs correctly: Use unique URIs to identify resources and follow a consistent URI pattern for all resources and relationships.
- Use HTTP methods and status codes correctly: Use the appropriate HTTP method for each operation and the appropriate HTTP status code to indicate the success or failure of each operation.
- Use consistent data formats: Use a consistent data format, such as JSON or XML, for all resource representations and relationships.
- Use pagination and filtering: Use pagination and filtering to retrieve related resources efficiently.
- Use caching: Use caching mechanisms to improve performance and reduce server load.

By following these best practices, developers can create RESTful APIs that efficiently and effectively handle relationships between resources.

In conclusion, handling relationships between resources is an important aspect of building a RESTful API. By following best practices for handling one-to-one, one-to-many, and many-to-many relationships, developers can create APIs that are efficient, maintainable, and scalable.

18

Pagination, Filtering, and Sorting

When working with large datasets in a RESTful API, it is important to provide mechanisms for clients to efficiently retrieve and manipulate the data. Pagination, filtering, and sorting are common techniques used to achieve this goal. In this section, we will explore how to implement pagination, filtering, and sorting in a RESTful API.

Pagination

Pagination is the process of dividing a large dataset into smaller pages to improve performance and reduce the amount of data transferred between the server and the client. In a RESTful API, pagination is typically implemented using the **limit** and **offset** query parameters.

The **limit** parameter specifies the maximum number of

resources to return in a single page, while the **offset** parameter specifies the starting point of the page. For example, to retrieve the first 10 resources of a collection, the following request can be made:

```
GET /resources?limit=10&offset=0
```

To retrieve the next 10 resources, the **offset** parameter can be updated to 10:

```
GET /resources?limit=10&offset=10
```

The server can return a response containing only the requested resources:

```
HTTP/1.1 200 OK
Content-Type: application/json

{
  "data": [
    {...},
    {...},
    {...},
    ...
  ],
  "meta": {
    "total": 100,
    "limit": 10,
    "offset": 10
  }
}
```

The **meta** object contains information about the pagination, including the total number of resources, the **limit** and **offset** values used, and any other relevant information.

Filtering

Filtering is the process of selecting a subset of resources based on specific criteria. In a RESTful API, filtering is typically implemented using query parameters that specify the filtering criteria.

For example, to retrieve all resources that match a certain value, the following request can be made:

```
GET /resources?filter=value
```

The server can return a response containing only the requested resources:

```
HTTP/1.1 200 OK
Content-Type: application/json

{
  "data": [
    {...},
    {...},
    {...},
    ...
  ],
  "meta": {
    "total": 50
```

```
    }
}
```

The **meta** object contains information about the number of resources that match the filtering criteria.

Sorting

Sorting is the process of arranging resources in a specific order based on one or more criteria. In a RESTful API, sorting is typically implemented using query parameters that specify the sorting criteria.

For example, to retrieve resources sorted by a certain field in ascending order, the following request can be made:

```
GET /resources?sort=field
```

To retrieve resources sorted by a certain field in descending order, the following request can be made:

```
GET /resources?sort=-field
```

The server can return a response containing the requested resources in the specified order:

```
HTTP/1.1 200 OK
Content-Type: application/json
```

```
{
  "data": [
    {...},
    {...},
    {...},
    ...
  ],
  "meta": {
    "total": 50
  }
}
```

The **meta** object contains information about the number of resources that were sorted.

Best Practices for Pagination, Filtering, and Sorting

When implementing pagination, filtering, and sorting in a RESTful API, it is important to follow best practices to ensure that the API is efficient, maintainable, and scalable. The following are some best practices for pagination, filtering, and sorting:

- Use consistent query parameter names: Use consistent query parameter names for pagination, filtering, and sorting to make it easy for clients to use the API.
- Use default values: Use default values for pagination, filtering, and sorting to make the API more user-friendly.

161

- Use efficient algorithms: Use efficient algorithms to paginate, filter, and sort the data to minimize server load and improve performance.
- Use indexes: Use indexes to speed up filtering and sorting operations on large datasets.
- Use caching: Use caching mechanisms to improve performance and reduce server load.

By following these best practices, developers can create RESTful APIs that efficiently handle pagination, filtering, and sorting operations on large datasets.

In conclusion, pagination, filtering, and sorting are important techniques used to improve the performance and scalability of RESTful APIs when working with large datasets. By following best practices for pagination, filtering, and sorting, developers can create APIs that are efficient, maintainable, and scalable.

19

API Authentication and Authorization

A PI authentication and authorization are essential components of building a secure and reliable RESTful API. In this section, we will explore the various authentication and authorization methods available and the best practices for implementing them.

Authentication

Authentication is the process of verifying the identity of a user or client that is attempting to access a resource or perform an action. In a RESTful API, authentication is typically implemented using tokens, such as JSON Web Tokens (JWTs) or OAuth tokens.

JWTs are self-contained tokens that contain information about the user and any necessary authorization data. When a user logs in or requests access to a protected resource, the server generates a JWT and sends it to the client. The client then includes the JWT in the **Authorization** header of subsequent requests. The server can decode and verify the JWT to determine the user's identity and authorize the requested action.

OAuth is an open standard for token-based authentication and authorization. OAuth allows third-party applications to access a user's resources without requiring the user to provide their username and password to the third-party application. OAuth tokens are short-lived tokens that grant access to specific resources or actions. The user authorizes the third-party application to access their resources, and the third-party application receives an OAuth token that can be used to authenticate and authorize future requests.

Authorization

Authorization is the process of determining whether a user or client is allowed to perform a specific action or access a specific resource. In a RESTful API, authorization is typically implemented using roles or permissions.

Roles are a collection of permissions that define the actions that a user or client is allowed to perform. Roles can be assigned to individual users or to groups of users. For example, an API may define an "admin" role that allows users to perform administrative actions, such as creating or deleting resources, while a "user" role may only allow users to view or update their own resources.

Permissions are individual rules that define the actions that a user or client is allowed to perform on a specific resource. For example, a user may be allowed to view a resource but not update or delete it.

Best Practices for Authentication and Authorization

When implementing authentication and authorization in a RESTful API, it is important to follow best practices to ensure that the API is secure, reliable, and user-friendly. The following are some best practices for authentication and authorization:

- Use secure token-based authentication: Use secure token-based authentication, such as JWT or OAuth, to authenticate users and clients.
- Use SSL/TLS: Use SSL/TLS to encrypt communication between the client and server to prevent eavesdropping and man-in-the-middle attacks.
- Use strong passwords: Use strong passwords and password policies to prevent unauthorized access to user accounts.
- Implement rate limiting: Implement rate limiting to prevent brute force attacks and protect against Denial-of-Service (DoS) attacks.
- Use role-based access control: Use role-based access control to define the actions that users or clients are allowed to perform.
- Use granular permissions: Use granular permissions to

provide fine-grained control over access to resources.
· Audit and log authentication and authorization events: Audit and log authentication and authorization events to detect and prevent unauthorized access.

By following these best practices, developers can create RESTful APIs that are secure, reliable, and user-friendly.

In conclusion, authentication and authorization are essential components of building a secure and reliable RESTful API. By using secure token-based authentication, implementing SSL/TLS, using strong passwords, implementing rate limiting, using role-based access control and granular permissions, and auditing and logging authentication and authorization events, developers can create APIs that are secure, reliable, and user-friendly.

Testing and Debugging a RESTful API

Testing and debugging are critical steps in the development of a RESTful API. In this section, we will explore the various techniques and tools available for testing and debugging a RESTful API.

Unit Testing

Unit testing is the process of testing individual components of an API in isolation to ensure that they are functioning as expected. In a RESTful API, unit testing is typically performed on the API endpoints and their associated logic. Unit tests are typically automated and run on a continuous integration server to ensure that the API is always functioning correctly.

To perform unit testing on an API endpoint, developers can create test cases that simulate requests to the endpoint with various inputs and verify that the responses are correct. For example, to test a **GET /resources** endpoint, developers can create test cases that verify that the endpoint returns the correct resources with the correct pagination, filtering, and sorting.

Unit tests can be written in a variety of programming languages, and there are many testing frameworks available that make it easy to create and run tests. Some popular testing frameworks for RESTful APIs include:

- PHPUnit (for PHP)
- Jest (for JavaScript)
- JUnit (for Java)
- PyTest (for Python)

Integration Testing

Integration testing is the process of testing the interaction between multiple components of an API to ensure that they are functioning correctly together. In a RESTful API, integration testing is typically performed on the API endpoints and their associated logic, as well as any third-party dependencies, such as databases or other APIs.

To perform integration testing on an API endpoint, developers can create test cases that simulate requests to the endpoint with various inputs and verify that the responses are correct. Integration tests can also verify that the API is correctly interacting with any third-party dependencies.

Integration tests can be more complex than unit tests, as they involve testing multiple components together. However, they are important for ensuring that the API is functioning correctly in a real-world environment.

Debugging

Debugging is the process of identifying and fixing errors in an API. In a RESTful API, debugging can involve analyzing server logs, inspecting network traffic, and using debugging tools.

One common debugging tool for RESTful APIs is the Postman app, which allows developers to easily create and send requests to an API and inspect the responses. Postman also includes a variety of debugging tools, such as a console for viewing server logs and an interface for inspecting network traffic.

Other debugging tools for RESTful APIs include:

- Wireshark: A network protocol analyzer that can capture and display network traffic.
- Chrome DevTools: A set of debugging tools built into the Chrome browser that can be used to inspect network traffic and analyze JavaScript code.
- Charles Proxy: A web debugging proxy that can capture and display network traffic between the client and server.

By using these tools and techniques, developers can test and debug their RESTful APIs to ensure that they are functioning correctly and reliably.

In conclusion, testing and debugging are critical steps in the development of a RESTful API. By using unit testing, integration testing, and debugging tools, developers can ensure that their APIs are functioning correctly and reliably.

20

Implementing HATEOAS

HATEOAS (Hypermedia as the Engine of Application State) is a constraint of the REST architectural style that enables a client to dynamically navigate an API by following links between resources. In this section, we will explore the benefits of HATEOAS and how to implement it in a RESTful API.

Benefits of HATEOAS

HATEOAS enables clients to interact with an API by following links between resources, rather than having to rely on a fixed set of endpoints. This makes APIs more flexible and adaptable, as clients can dynamically navigate the API based on the available resources and their relationships.

HATEOAS also makes APIs more discoverable, as clients can explore the available resources and their relationships through the links provided by the API. This can make APIs more user-friendly, as clients can easily find and access the resources they need.

Finally, HATEOAS can simplify API development and maintenance, as it allows developers to focus on defining the resources and their relationships, rather than having to define a fixed set of endpoints. This can make APIs more adaptable to changing requirements and reduce the amount of code that needs to be maintained.

Implementing HATEOAS

To implement HATEOAS in a RESTful API, developers need to define the resources and their relationships, and provide links between the resources in the API responses. This can be done using a variety of formats, such as HAL (Hypertext Application Language), JSON-LD (JSON Linked Data), or Siren.

HAL is a simple format for defining hypermedia APIs that is based on JSON. In HAL, each resource is represented as a JSON object that includes links to other resources, as well as any other relevant information. Here is an example of a HAL resource:

```
{
  "name": "John Doe",
  "age": 30,
  "_links": {
    "self": {
```

```
      "href": "/users/123"
    },
    "friends": {
      "href": "/users/123/friends"
    }
  }
}
```

In this example, the resource represents a user with the name "John Doe" and age 30. The resource also includes links to itself (**/users/123**) and the user's friends (**/users/123/friends**).

JSON-LD is a more complex format for defining hypermedia APIs that is based on JSON-LD. JSON-LD allows developers to define a vocabulary for their API, and represent resources and their relationships using linked data. Here is an example of a JSON-LD resource:

```
{
  "@context": "http://schema.org",
  "@type": "Person",
  "name": "John Doe",
  "age": 30,
  "@id": "/users/123",
  "knows": {
    "@id": "/users/456",
    "@type": "Person",
    "name": "Jane Smith"
  }
}
```

In this example, the resource represents a person with the name "John Doe" and age 30. The resource includes a link to itself (**/users/123**), and a relationship with another person named "Jane Smith" (**/users/456**).

Siren is a format for defining hypermedia APIs that is based on JSON. Siren allows developers to define resources and their relationships using a set of predefined classes, such as **entity**, **link**, and **action**. Here is an example of a Siren resource:

```
{
"class": ["person"],
"properties": {
"name": "John Doe",
"age": 30
},
"links": [
{"
rel": ["self"], "href": "/users/123" },
{ "rel": ["friends"], "href": "/users/123/friends"
} ]
}
```

In this example, the resource represents a person with the name "John Doe" and age 30. The resource is defined using the 'person' class, and includes links to itself ('/users/123') and the user's friends ('/users/123/friends').

To implement HATEOAS in a RESTful API, developers need to define the resources and their relationships using a hypermedia format such as HAL, JSON-LD, or Siren, and provide links between the resources in the API responses. This can be done using a variety of tools and libraries, such as the Spring HATEOAS library for Java or the Flask-HAL library for Python.

In conclusion, HATEOAS is a powerful constraint of the

REST architectural style that enables clients to dynamically navigate a RESTful API by following links between resources. By implementing HATEOAS in a RESTful API, developers can make their APIs more flexible, adaptable, and discoverable, and simplify API development and maintenance.

21

Testing and Debugging

Testing and debugging are critical steps in the development of a RESTful API. In this section, we will explore the various techniques and tools available for testing and debugging a RESTful API.

Unit Testing

Unit testing is the process of testing individual components of an API in isolation to ensure that they are functioning as expected. In a RESTful API, unit testing is typically performed on the API endpoints and their associated logic. Unit tests are typically automated and run on a continuous integration server to ensure that the API is always functioning correctly.

To perform unit testing on an API endpoint, developers can create test cases that simulate requests to the endpoint with various inputs and verify that the responses are correct.

For example, to test a **GET /resources** endpoint, developers can create test cases that verify that the endpoint returns the correct resources with the correct pagination, filtering, and sorting.

Unit tests can be written in a variety of programming languages, and there are many testing frameworks available that make it easy to create and run tests. Some popular testing frameworks for RESTful APIs include:

- PHPUnit (for PHP)
- Jest (for JavaScript)
- JUnit (for Java)
- PyTest (for Python)

Integration Testing

Integration testing is the process of testing the interaction between multiple components of an API to ensure that they are functioning correctly together. In a RESTful API, integration testing is typically performed on the API endpoints and their associated logic, as well as any third-party dependencies, such as databases or other APIs.

To perform integration testing on an API endpoint, developers can create test cases that simulate requests to the endpoint with various inputs and verify that the responses are correct. Integration tests can also verify that the API is correctly interacting with any third-party dependencies.

Integration tests can be more complex than unit tests, as they involve testing multiple components together. However, they are important for ensuring that the API is functioning correctly in a real-world environment.

Debugging

Debugging is the process of identifying and fixing errors in an API. In a RESTful API, debugging can involve analyzing server logs, inspecting network traffic, and using debugging tools.

One common debugging tool for RESTful APIs is the Post-man app, which allows developers to easily create and send requests to an API and inspect the responses. Postman also includes a variety of debugging tools, such as a console for viewing server logs and an interface for inspecting network traffic.

Other debugging tools for RESTful APIs include:

- Wireshark: A network protocol analyzer that can capture and display network traffic.
- Chrome DevTools: A set of debugging tools built into the Chrome browser that can be used to inspect network traffic and analyze JavaScript code.
- Charles Proxy: A web debugging proxy that can capture and display network traffic between the client and server.

By using these tools and techniques, developers can test and debug their RESTful APIs to ensure that they are functioning correctly and reliably.

In conclusion, testing and debugging are critical steps in the development of a RESTful API. By using unit testing, integration testing, and debugging tools, developers can ensure that their APIs are functioning correctly and reliably.

IV

Building a GraphQL API

GraphQL is a query language and runtime for APIs that was developed by Facebook. In this chapter, we will explore the concepts and principles behind GraphQL and how to build a GraphQL API.

22

GraphQL Concepts

G raphQL is a query language and runtime for APIs that allows clients to request exactly the data they need and nothing more. In a GraphQL API, clients send queries to the server that specify the data they need, and the server returns a JSON response that includes only that data.

GraphQL has several key concepts that are important to understand when building a GraphQL API:

Schema

The schema is the core of a GraphQL API. The schema defines the types of data that can be queried, and the relationships between those types. The schema is typically defined using the GraphQL Schema Definition Language (SDL), which is a simple syntax for defining types and fields.

Here is an example of a simple GraphQL schema:

```
type Query {
  hello: String
}
```

In this example, the schema defines a single type **Query** with a single field **hello** that returns a string.

Types

Types are the building blocks of a GraphQL API. In a GraphQL schema, types define the shape of the data that can be queried, and the relationships between that data. Types can be scalar types (like strings and integers), or object types (which can contain other types).

Here is an example of a GraphQL schema that defines an object type **User** with scalar fields **name** and **email**:

```
type User {
  name: String
  email: String
}
```

Fields

Fields are the properties of a type in a GraphQL schema. In a GraphQL query, fields are used to specify the data that the client wants to retrieve. Fields can be scalar fields (like strings and integers), or object fields (which represent other types).

Here is an example of a GraphQL query that retrieves the **name** and **email** fields for a **User**:

```
{
  user(id: "123") {
    name
    email
  }
}
```

In this example, the query specifies the **user** field with an argument **id** of "123", and requests the **name** and **email** fields for that user.

Queries

Queries are the requests that clients send to a GraphQL API to retrieve data. In a GraphQL query, clients specify the data they want to retrieve using fields and arguments.

Here is an example of a GraphQL query that retrieves the **name** and **email** fields for a **User**:

```
{
  user(id: "123") {
    name
    email
  }
}
```

In this example, the query specifies the **user** field with an argument **id** of "123", and requests the **name** and **email** fields for that user.

Mutations

Mutations are the requests that clients send to a GraphQL API to modify data. In a GraphQL mutation, clients specify the data they want to modify using input fields and arguments.

Here is an example of a GraphQL mutation that creates a new **User**:

```
mutation {
  createUser(input: { name: "John Doe", email:
  "john.doe@example.com" }) {
    id
    name
    email
  }
}
```

In this example, the mutation specifies the **createUser** field with an input argument that contains the **name** and **email** fields for the new user, and requests the **id**, **name**, and **email** fields for the newly created user.

Subscriptions

Subscriptions are a way for clients to receive real-time updates from a GraphQL API. In a GraphQL subscription, clients specify the data they want to receive updates for using fields and arguments, and the server pushes updates to the client when the data changes.

Here is an example of a GraphQL subscription that receives updates when a new **Comment** is posted:

```
subscription {
  commentAdded(postId: "123") {
    id
    content
    author {
      name
    }
  }
}
```

In this example, the subscription specifies the **commen-tAdded** field with an argument **postId** of "123", and requests the **id**, **content**, and **author** fields for new comments on that post.

Resolvers

Resolvers are the functions that execute the logic for each field in a GraphQL schema. In a resolver, developers specify how to retrieve or modify the data for that field. Resolvers can retrieve data from a database, call external APIs, or perform other operations as needed.

Here is an example of a resolver function that retrieves a user by ID:

```
function resolveUser(parent, args, context) {
  const { id } = args;
  return User.findById(id);
}
```

In this example, the resolver function takes three arguments: **parent**, **args**, and **context**. The **args** argument contains any arguments passed to the query or mutation, and the **User.findById(id)** method retrieves the user from a database.

In conclusion, GraphQL is a query language and runtime for APIs that allows clients to request exactly the data they need and nothing more. GraphQL has several key concepts, including the schema, types, fields, queries, mutations, subscriptions, and resolvers.

23

Defining GraphQL Schema

In a GraphQL API, the schema is the core of the system, as it defines the types of data that can be queried and the relationships between those types. In this section, we will explore how to define a GraphQL schema and the best practices for schema design.

Types

In a GraphQL schema, types define the shape of the data that can be queried and the relationships between that data. There are two main types of types in a GraphQL schema: scalar types and object types.

Scalar types represent primitive data types like strings, integers, and booleans. GraphQL has a number of built-in scalar types, including **String**, **Int**, **Float**, **Boolean**, and **ID**. Here is an example of a GraphQL schema that defines a scalar type:

```
scalar Date

type User {
  id: ID!
  name: String!
  email: String!
  createdAt: Date!
}
```

In this example, the **Date** scalar type represents a date value. The **User** object type defines three fields of scalar types (**name**, **email**, and **createdAt**) and one field of type **ID**.

Object types represent complex data types that can contain other types, including scalar types and other object types. Here is an example of a GraphQL schema that defines an object type:

```
type User {
  id: ID!
  name: String!
  email: String!
  posts: [Post!]!
}

type Post {
  id: ID!
  title: String!
  content: String!
  author: User!
}
```

In this example, the **User** object type has a field **posts** that is an array of **Post** object types. The **Post** object type has a field **author** that is a **User** object type.

Fields

Fields are the properties of a type in a GraphQL schema. In a GraphQL query, fields are used to specify the data that the client wants to retrieve. Fields can be scalar fields or object fields.

Here is an example of a GraphQL schema that defines a scalar field and an object field:

```
type User {
  id: ID!
  name: String!
  email: String!
  createdAt: Date!
  posts: [Post!]!
}

type Post {
  id: ID!
  title: String!
  content: String!
  author: User!
  createdAt: Date!
}
```

In this example, the **User** object type has a field **posts** that is an array of **Post** object types. The **Post** object type has a field **author** that is a **User** object type.

Queries

In a GraphQL API, clients send queries to the server to retrieve data. In a query, clients specify the data they want to retrieve using fields and arguments.

Here is an example of a GraphQL query that retrieves the **name**, **email**, and **createdAt** fields for a **User**:

```
{
  user(id: "123") {
    name
    email
    createdAt
  }
}
```

In this example, the query specifies the **user** field with an argument **id** of "123", and requests the **name**, **email**, and **createdAt** fields for that user.

Mutations

In a GraphQL API, clients can also send mutations to modify data. In a mutation, clients specify the data they want to modify using input fields and arguments.

Here is an example of a GraphQL mutation that creates a new **User**:

```
mutation {
  createUser(input: { name: "John Doe", email:
  "john.doe@example.com" }) {
    id
    name
    email
  }
}
```

In this example, the mutation specifies the **createUser** field with an input object that contains the **name** and **email** fields for the new user, and requests the **id**, **name**, and **email** fields for the created user.

Subscriptions

In a GraphQL API, clients can subscribe to receive real-time updates when data changes. In a subscription, clients specify the data they want to receive updates for using fields and arguments, and the server pushes updates to the client when the data changes.

Here is an example of a GraphQL subscription that receives updates when a new **Comment** is posted:

```
subscription {
  commentAdded(postId: "123") {
    id
    content
    author {
      name
    }
  }
}
```

In this example, the subscription specifies the **commentAdded** field with an argument **postId** of "123", and requests the **id**, **content**, and **author** fields for new comments on that post.

Schema Design Best Practices

When designing a GraphQL schema, there are several best practices that can help ensure the schema is easy to use and maintain:

- Define clear types with descriptive names: use clear and concise names for types and fields to make the schema easy to understand.

- Group fields logically: group fields that belong together under a single type.
- Use input types for mutations: use input types to group mutation input fields.
- Use interfaces and unions for polymorphic types: use interfaces and unions to define polymorphic types that can return multiple object types.
- Avoid circular dependencies: avoid creating circular dependencies between types.
- Document the schema: document the schema using comments or a separate documentation tool.

In conclusion, a GraphQL schema defines the types of data that can be queried and the relationships between those types. When designing a GraphQL schema, developers should follow best practices to ensure the schema is easy to use and maintain.

24

Implementing Queries and Mutations

I n a GraphQL API, queries and mutations define the operations that clients can perform on the data. In this section, we will explore how to implement queries and mutations in a GraphQL API using the Apollo Server library.

Setting up Apollo Server

To get started with Apollo Server, you will need to install the library using npm or yarn:

```
npm install apollo-server
```

Once you have installed the library, you can create a new instance of Apollo Server and define your GraphQL schema:

```
const { ApolloServer, gql } =
require('apollo-server');

const typeDefs = gql`
  type Query {
    hello: String
  }
`;

const resolvers = {
  Query: {
    hello: () => 'Hello world!',
  },
};

const server = new ApolloServer({ typeDefs,
resolvers });

server.listen().then(({ url }) => {
  console.log(`Server ready at ${url}`);
});
```

In this example, we define a simple **hello** query that returns the string "Hello world!". We define the query in our schema using the **gql** function, and we define the resolver for the query in the **resolvers** object.

We create a new instance of Apollo Server with our schema and resolvers, and we start the server with the **listen** method. Once the server is running, we log the URL where the server is available.

Implementing Queries

To implement a query in a GraphQL API, we need to define the query in our schema and implement the resolver for the query.

Here is an example of a GraphQL schema that defines a **user** query:

```
type Query {
  user(id: ID!): User
}

type User {
  id: ID!
  name: String!
  email: String!
}
```

In this example, the **user** query takes an argument **id** of type **ID!**, and returns a **User** object type.

To implement the **user** query, we need to define a resolver function that retrieves the user from a database:

```
const resolvers = {
  Query: {
    user: (parent, args, context) => {
      const { id } = args;
      return User.findById(id);
    },
  },
};
```

196

In this example, the resolver function takes three arguments: **parent**, **args**, and **context**. The **args** argument contains the **id** argument passed to the query, and the **User.findById(id)** method retrieves the user from a database.

Implementing Mutations

To implement a mutation in a GraphQL API, we need to define the mutation in our schema and implement the resolver for the mutation.

Here is an example of a GraphQL schema that defines a **createUser** mutation:

```
type Mutation {
  createUser(input: CreateUserInput!): User!
}

input CreateUserInput {
  name: String!
  email: String!
}

type User {
  id: ID!
  name: String!
  email: String!
}
```

In this example, the **createUser** mutation takes an input object of type **CreateUserInput**, and returns a **User** object type.

197

To implement the **createUser** mutation, we need to define a resolver function that creates a new user in a database:

```
const resolvers = {
  Mutation: {
    createUser: (parent, args, context) => {
      const { input } = args;
      const user = new User(input);
      return user.save();
    },
  },
};
```

In this example, the resolver function takes three arguments: **parent**, **args**, and context. The **args** argument contains the **input** argument passed to the mutation, and we create a new user object with the input fields using the **User** constructor. We save the user to the database with the **user.save()** method and return the saved user.

Error Handling

In a GraphQL API, errors can occur at different levels: schema validation, resolver execution, and data fetching. Apollo Server provides a built-in error handling mechanism that handles errors and returns them to the client in a standardized format.

To handle errors in a GraphQL API, we can define error handling middleware in Apollo Server:

```
const server = new ApolloServer({
  typeDefs,
  resolvers,
  formatError: (error) => {
    console.log(error);
    return error;
  },
});
```

In this example, we define a **formatError** function that logs the error to the console and returns the error object. The **formatError** function can be used to customize the error format returned to the client.

Caching

In a GraphQL API, caching can improve performance by reducing the number of requests to the data source. Apollo Server provides a built-in caching mechanism that caches the results of queries and mutations.

To enable caching in Apollo Server, we can use the **apollo-server-caching** package and add a cache implementation to the server:

```
const { ApolloServer, gql } =
require('apollo-server');
const RedisCache =
require('apollo-server-cache-redis');
```

```
const typeDefs = gql`
  type Query {
    user(id: ID!): User
  }

  type User {
    id: ID!
    name: String!
    email: String!
  }
`;

const resolvers = {
  Query: {
    user: (parent, args, context) => {
      const { id } = args;
      return
      context.dataSources.userAPI.getUser(id);
    },
  },
};

const server = new ApolloServer({
  typeDefs,
  resolvers,
  cache: new RedisCache({
    host: 'localhost',
    port: 6379,
  }),
  dataSources: () => ({
    userAPI: new UserAPI(),
  }),
});

server.listen().then(({ url }) => {
  console.log(`Server ready at ${url}`);
```

```
});
```

In this example, we use the **RedisCache** implementation from the **apollo-server-caching** package to cache the results of queries and mutations. We add the cache implementation to the server with the **cache** option.

We also define a **dataSources** function that creates a new instance of the **UserAPI** data source. The data source is used in the resolver function to retrieve the user from the data source, and the results are cached by the cache implementation.

In conclusion, Apollo Server provides a powerful framework for building GraphQL APIs with JavaScript. With Apollo Server, developers can easily define their GraphQL schema, implement queries and mutations, handle errors, and enable caching. In the next chapter, we will explore how to consume APIs with client applications.

25

Handling Real-time Updates with Subscriptions

In a GraphQL API, subscriptions allow clients to receive real-time updates from the server when the data changes. Subscriptions are a powerful feature that can be used to build real-time applications such as chat applications, social networks, and gaming platforms.

Subscriptions in GraphQL

Subscriptions in GraphQL are similar to queries and mutations, but instead of returning a single result, they return a stream of results that are sent to the client over a WebSocket connection. Subscriptions are defined in the schema with a special **Subscription** object type, and the subscription resolver function returns an **AsyncIterator** object that emits the updates.

Here is an example of a subscription that returns real-time updates for a chat application:

```
type Subscription {
  messageAdded(roomId: ID!): Message
}

type Message {
  id: ID!
  text: String!
  user: User!
  createdAt: DateTime!
}

type User {
  id: ID!
  name: String!
  avatarUrl: String!
}

scalar DateTime
```

In this example, the **messageAdded** subscription takes an argument **roomId** of type **ID!**, and returns a **Message** object type.

To implement the **messageAdded** subscription, we need to define a subscription resolver function that returns an **AsyncIterator** object that emits the updates:

```
const resolvers = {
  Subscription: {
    messageAdded: {
      subscribe: withFilter(
        () => pubsub.asyncIterator('MESSAGE_ADDED'),
```

```
      (payload, variables) => {
        return payload.roomId ===
        variables.roomId;
      },
    ),
  },
 },
};
```

In this example, we use the **withFilter** function from the **graphql-subscriptions** library to filter the updates based on the **roomId** argument passed by the client.

The subscription resolver function returns an **AsyncIterator** object that listens for updates on the **MESSAGE_ADDED** channel. The **withFilter** function filters the updates based on the **roomId** argument, and returns only the updates that match the filter.

Setting up a Subscription Server

To enable subscriptions in a GraphQL API, we need to set up a subscription server that listens for WebSocket connections and handles the subscription requests.

In Apollo Server, we can set up a subscription server by using the **createServer** function from the **http** library, and passing it to the **listen** method of the Apollo Server instance:

```
const httpServer = http.createServer(app);

server.listen({ httpServer }, () => {
  console.log(`Server ready at
  http://localhost:${PORT}${server.graphqlPath}`);
  console.log(`Subscriptions ready at
  ws://localhost:${PORT}${server.subscriptionsPath}`);
});
```

In this example, we create an HTTP server using the **createServer** function from the **http** library, and pass it to the
httpServer option of the **listen** method. We log the URL
where the server is available, as well as the URL where the
subscription server is available.

Client-side Subscriptions

To consume subscriptions in a client application, we need to
use a WebSocket client library that supports subscriptions.
In a JavaScript application, we can use the **subscriptions-
transport-ws** library to handle subscriptions.

Here is an example of how to use the **subscriptions-
transport-ws** library to subscribe to a **messageAdded**
subscription in a React component:

```
import { useSubscription } from '@apollo/client';
import { messageAdded } from './subscription';

function MessageList() {
```

205

```
const { data } = useSubscription(messageAdded, {
  variables: { roomId: '123' },
});
```

In this example, we use the **useSubscription** hook from the **@apollo/client** library to subscribe to the **messageAdded** subscription. We pass the **messageAdded** subscription definition as the first argument, and the subscription variables as the second argument.

The hook returns a **data** object that contains the updates received from the server.

Scaling Subscriptions

Subscriptions can be challenging to scale because they require a persistent WebSocket connection between the client and the server. To handle a large number of WebSocket connections, we need to use a WebSocket server that can handle thousands of connections simultaneously.

One way to scale subscriptions is to use a WebSocket server such as **WebSocket** or **Socket.IO** to handle the WebSocket connections, and use a message queue such as **Redis** or **RabbitMQ** to handle the updates.

In this architecture, the WebSocket server listens for WebSocket connections and sends the subscription requests to the message queue. The subscription resolver function listens for updates on the message queue, and sends the updates to the WebSocket server, which in turn sends the updates to the client over the WebSocket connection.

Subscription Security

Subscriptions can pose a security risk if they are not properly secured. An attacker can use a subscription to consume large amounts of server resources, or to listen for sensitive data.

To secure subscriptions in a GraphQL API, we can use authentication and authorization to ensure that only authorized users can subscribe to sensitive data.

In addition, we can limit the rate of subscriptions to prevent an attacker from consuming too many server resources. We can use a rate limiting middleware such as **graphql-rate-limit** to limit the number of subscriptions per user or per IP address.

In conclusion, subscriptions are a powerful feature that allow clients to receive real-time updates from a GraphQL API. With subscriptions, we can build real-time applications such as chat applications, social networks, and gaming platforms. To implement subscriptions in a GraphQL API, we need to set up a subscription server, define subscription resolvers, and use a WebSocket client library to consume the subscriptions in a client application. Subscriptions can pose a security risk if they are not properly secured, so it is important to use authentication, authorization, and rate limiting to secure subscriptions in a GraphQL API.

26

API Authentication and Authorization

A PI authentication and authorization are essential components of building secure and scalable APIs. In this chapter, we will cover different authentication and authorization strategies and their implementation in an API.

Authentication Strategies

There are several authentication strategies to choose from, each with its own benefits and drawbacks. Some of the most common authentication strategies include:

- Token-based authentication: In token-based authentication, a client sends a token, such as a JSON Web Token (JWT), with each request to authenticate the user. The server validates the token and authorizes the user if the token is valid.

- OAuth 2.0: OAuth 2.0 is an authentication protocol that allows users to grant third-party applications access to their resources on a server without sharing their credentials. OAuth 2.0 uses access tokens to authenticate the user.
- Basic authentication: In basic authentication, a client sends the username and password with each request to authenticate the user. The server validates the credentials and authorizes the user if the credentials are valid.

Authorization Strategies

Authorization determines what a user can and cannot access in an API. There are several authorization strategies to choose from, each with its own benefits and drawbacks. Some of the most common authorization strategies include:

- Role-based access control (RBAC): In RBAC, users are assigned roles that define what resources they can access. The server checks the user's role to determine if they are authorized to access a resource.
- Attribute-based access control (ABAC): In ABAC, users are assigned attributes that define their characteristics. The server checks the user's attributes to determine if they are authorized to access a resource.
- Policy-based access control: In policy-based access con-

trol, access control policies define what resources a user can access based on a set of rules. The server checks the policies to determine if a user is authorized to access a resource.

Implementation in an API

To implement authentication and authorization in an API, we need to define an authentication and authorization mechanism and integrate it with the API. Some common implementation patterns include:

- Middleware: In middleware-based authentication and authorization, the API uses a middleware function to authenticate and authorize the user before handling the request. The middleware function checks the user's credentials or token and determines if they are authorized to access the requested resource.
- Authentication and authorization server: In an authentication and authorization server-based implementation, the API delegates authentication and authorization to an external server. The client sends a request to the authentication and authorization server to authenticate the user and retrieve a token, which is used to authenticate and authorize the user in subsequent requests.

In conclusion, authentication and authorization are essential components of building secure and scalable APIs. There are several authentication and authorization strategies to choose from, each with its own benefits and drawbacks. To implement authentication and authorization in an API, we need to define an authentication and authorization mechanism and integrate it with the API.

27

Error Handling and Validation

E rror handling and validation are critical components of building reliable and robust APIs. In this chapter, we will cover different error handling and validation strategies and their implementation in an API.

Error Handling Strategies

There are several error handling strategies to choose from, each with its own benefits and drawbacks. Some of the most common error handling strategies include:

- Return errors as JSON: In this strategy, the API returns error responses as JSON objects that contain an error message and status code. The client can use the error message to diagnose the problem and take corrective action.

Use HTTP status codes: In this strategy, the API uses HTTP status codes to indicate the status of the request. For example, a 404 status code can be used to indicate that the requested resource was not found, while a 500 status code can be used to indicate a server error.

- Include error details in response headers: In this strategy, the API includes error details in the response headers. This can be useful for debugging purposes.

Validation Strategies

Validation ensures that the data sent to the API is correct and meets the required criteria. There are several validation strategies to choose from, each with its own benefits and drawbacks. Some of the most common validation strategies include:

- Use JSON Schema: In this strategy, the API defines a JSON Schema that describes the expected structure and format of the request and response data. The API validates the data against the JSON Schema to ensure that it is correct.
- Use data annotations: In this strategy, the API uses data annotations to define the required data format and validation rules. The API validates the data against the data annotations to ensure that it is correct.
- Use a validation library: In this strategy, the API uses a validation library, such as Joi or Yup, to validate the data.

The validation library provides a set of validation rules and functions that can be used to validate the data.

Implementation in an API

To implement error handling and validation in an API, we need to define an error handling and validation mechanism and integrate it with the API. Some common implementation patterns include:

- Middleware: In middleware-based error handling and validation, the API uses a middleware function to validate the request data and handle errors. The middleware function checks the data against the validation rules and returns an error response if the data is invalid.
- Use a validation library: In library-based validation, the API uses a validation library to validate the request data. The library provides a set of validation rules and functions that can be used to validate the data.

In conclusion, error handling and validation are critical components of building reliable and robust APIs. There are several error handling and validation strategies to choose from, each with its own benefits and drawbacks. To implement error handling and validation in an API, we need to define an error handling and validation mechanism and integrate it with the API.

28

Performance Optimization

Performance optimization is essential for building fast and scalable APIs. In this chapter, we will cover different performance optimization strategies and their implementation in an API.

Caching

Caching is a technique that can significantly improve API performance by storing frequently accessed data in memory. There are several caching strategies to choose from, each with its own benefits and drawbacks. Some of the most common caching strategies include:

- In-memory caching: In this strategy, the API stores frequently accessed data in memory. This can significantly reduce the response time for subsequent requests.

- Distributed caching: In this strategy, the API uses a distributed cache, such as Redis or Memcached, to store frequently accessed data. This can improve the scalability of the API by allowing multiple instances of the API to share the same cache.
- Client-side caching: In this strategy, the API uses HTTP caching headers to instruct the client to cache the response. This can significantly reduce the number of requests sent to the API and improve the response time.

Load Balancing

Load balancing is a technique that can improve API performance by distributing the workload across multiple servers. There are several load balancing strategies to choose from, each with its own benefits and drawbacks. Some of the most common load balancing strategies include:

- Round-robin load balancing: In this strategy, requests are distributed to servers in a round-robin fashion. This can ensure that the workload is evenly distributed across all servers.

Least connections load balancing: In this strategy, requests are distributed to servers with the least number of active connections. This can ensure that the workload is distributed to the servers with the most available resources.

- IP hash load balancing: In this strategy, requests are distributed to servers based on their IP address. This can ensure that requests from the same client are always sent to the same server, which can be useful for maintaining session state.

API Design

The design of the API can also impact its performance. Some tips for designing high-performance APIs include:

- Use pagination: If the API returns a large number of results, it is a good idea to use pagination to limit the number of results returned in each request. This can improve the response time and reduce the load on the server.
- Minimize the number of requests: It is important to minimize the number of requests required to complete a task. This can be achieved by designing the API to accept multiple parameters in a single request, or by providing batch processing capabilities.
- Use efficient data formats: The data format used by the API can also impact its performance. It is important to choose a data format that is efficient and easy to parse, such as JSON or Protocol Buffers.

Implementation in an API

To implement performance optimization in an API, we need to identify the performance bottlenecks and implement the appropriate optimization strategies. Some common implementation patterns include:

- Use a caching layer: To implement caching, we can use a caching layer, such as Redis or Memcached. The API can store frequently accessed data in the cache, which can significantly improve the response time.
- Use a load balancer: To implement load balancing, we can use a load balancer, such as NGINX or HAProxy. The load balancer can distribute the workload across multiple servers, which can improve the scalability and availability of the API.
- Optimize database queries: To improve the performance of database queries, we can optimize the queries themselves or use a database caching layer, such as Amazon ElastiCache or Redis.

In conclusion, performance optimization is essential for building fast and scalable APIs. There are several performance optimization strategies to choose from, each with its own benefits and drawbacks. To implement performance optimization in an API, we need to identify the performance bottlenecks and implement the appropriate optimization strategies.

V

Building a SOAP API

29

SOAP Protocol Basics

The Simple Object Access Protocol (SOAP) is a messaging protocol used for exchanging structured data between applications over the internet. SOAP is a protocol that uses XML-based messages to provide a standardized way for applications to communicate with each other. In this section, we will explore the basics of the SOAP protocol, including its structure, messaging model, and features.

SOAP Structure

A SOAP message is a structured XML document that contains a header, a body, and an optional fault element. The header contains any additional information that needs to be trans-mitted along with the message, such as authentication details, routing information, or message metadata. The body contains the actual data being transmitted between the applications.

The SOAP envelope is the top-level element in a SOAP message and is responsible for defining the structure of the message. The SOAP envelope contains the following elements:

- SOAP header: The SOAP header is an optional element that contains any additional information that needs to be transmitted along with the message.
- SOAP body: The SOAP body contains the actual data being transmitted between the applications.
- SOAP fault: The SOAP fault element is used to indicate an error in the message transmission or processing.

SOAP Messaging Model

The SOAP messaging model is based on the exchange of messages between a sender and a receiver. The sender constructs a SOAP message and sends it to the receiver, which processes the message and sends a response back to the sender. The messaging model can be either synchronous or asynchronous.

In a synchronous messaging model, the sender waits for a response from the receiver before proceeding with its processing. In an asynchronous messaging model, the sender does not wait for a response and continues with its processing. Asynchronous messaging can be useful in situations where the processing time for a message is long or where the receiver is not immediately available.

SOAP Features

SOAP provides several features that make it a popular protocol for building distributed applications. Some of these features include:

- Extensibility: SOAP is an extensible protocol that allows additional functionality to be added as needed.
- Platform independence: SOAP is platform-independent and can be used with any programming language or operating system.
- Interoperability: SOAP messages can be exchanged between different platforms and programming languages, making it a useful protocol for building distributed applications.
- Security: SOAP provides several security mechanisms, such as XML Signature and XML Encryption, that can be used to secure the communication between applications.
- Reliability: SOAP provides mechanisms for ensuring the reliable delivery of messages, such as message acknowledgement and retry mechanisms.

In conclusion, the SOAP protocol is a messaging protocol used for exchanging structured data between applications over the internet. SOAP is based on the exchange of messages between a sender and a receiver and provides several features that make it a popular protocol for building distributed applications, including extensibility, platform independence, interoperability, security, and reliability.

30

Defining WSDL (Web Services Description Language)

Web Services Description Language (WSDL) is an XML-based language used to describe the functionality offered by a web service. A WSDL document defines the operations provided by a web service, the input and output parameters for each operation, and the protocols used for communication. In this section, we will explore the basics of WSDL and how it is used in SOAP APIs.

WSDL is typically used in conjunction with SOAP to define the interface of a web service. A WSDL document contains the following elements:

- Types: The types element defines the data types used by the web service. The types can be defined using XML Schema, which provides a way to define the structure and content of the data.
- Messages: The messages element defines the data being exchanged between the web service and the client. A message can contain one or more parts, each with its own

data type.

- Operations: The operations element defines the operations provided by the web service. Each operation specifies the input and output messages, as well as any fault messages that can be returned in the event of an error.
- PortType: The portType element defines a set of operations that can be performed by the web service. Each operation is defined as a combination of input and output messages.
- Binding: The binding element defines the protocol used for communication between the web service and the client. A binding specifies the portType, the encoding format, and the transport protocol used to communicate with the web service.
- Service: The service element defines the endpoint of the web service. It specifies the port used for communication, the binding used, and the location of the WSDL document.

WSDL provides a standardized way to describe the functionality offered by a web service, which makes it easier for clients to consume the service. The WSDL document can be used to generate client-side code that can be used to invoke the web service. This makes it easier for clients to consume the web service, as they do not need to manually construct SOAP messages.

In conclusion, WSDL is an XML-based language used to describe the functionality offered by a web service. A WSDL document defines the operations provided by a web service, the input and output parameters for each operation, and the protocols used for communication. WSDL provides a standardized way to describe the functionality offered by a web service, which makes it easier for clients to consume the service.

31

Implementing SOAP Services

S OAP services can be implemented using a variety
of programming languages and platforms. In this
section, we will explore the basics of implementing
SOAP services using Java and .NET.

Implementing SOAP Services in Java

Java provides several APIs for implementing SOAP services,
including Java API for XML-Based Web Services (JAX-WS) and
Simple Object Access Protocol (SOAP) with Attachments API
for Java (SAAJ). JAX-WS provides a high-level API for building
SOAP web services, while SAAJ provides a low-level API for
working with SOAP messages directly.

To implement a SOAP service using JAX-WS, you need to
define a service endpoint interface (SEI) that specifies the
operations provided by the service. The SEI can be annotated

with the @WebService annotation, which indicates that the interface defines a web service. The @WebMethod annotation is used to specify the individual operations provided by the service.

Here is an example of a simple web service implemented using JAX-WS:

```
@WebService
public interface HelloWorld {
    @WebMethod
    String sayHello(String name);
}

@WebService(endpointInterface =
"com.example.HelloWorld")
public class HelloWorldImpl implements HelloWorld {
    public String sayHello(String name) {
        return "Hello " + name + "!";
    }
}
```

In this example, we define a simple web service that takes a name as input and returns a greeting. The web service is implemented as a Java class that implements the HelloWorld interface. The @WebService and @WebMethod annotations are used to specify that the interface defines a web service and to specify the individual operations provided by the service.

To deploy the web service, you need to package the service into a WAR file and deploy it to a web server such as Apache Tomcat. Once the web service is deployed, clients can access the service using a SOAP client such as the Java API for XML-Based RPC (JAX-RPC).

Implementing SOAP Services in .NET

Microsoft .NET provides several APIs for implementing SOAP services, including Windows Communication Foundation (WCF) and ASP.NET Web Services. WCF is a powerful and flexible framework for building distributed applications, while ASP.NET Web Services provides a simpler API for building SOAP services.

To implement a SOAP service using ASP.NET Web Services, you need to define a web service class that inherits from the System.Web.Services.WebService class. The web service class contains the individual methods provided by the service.

Here is an example of a simple web service implemented using ASP.NET Web Services:

```
[WebService(Namespace = "http://tempuri.org/")]
[WebServiceBinding(ConformsTo =
WsiProfiles.BasicProfile1_1)]
public class HelloWorld :
System.Web.Services.WebService {
    [WebMethod]
    public string SayHello(string name) {
        return "Hello " + name + "!";
    }
}
```

In this example, we define a simple web service that takes a name as input and returns a greeting. The web service is implemented as a C# class that inherits from the System.Web.Services.WebService class. The [WebService] and [WebMethod] attributes are used to specify that the class defines a web service and to specify the individual methods provided by the service.

To deploy the web service, you need to compile the service into a DLL file and deploy it to a web server such as Microsoft Internet Information Services (IIS). Once the web service is deployed, clients can access the service using a SOAP client such as Microsoft .NET Framework.

Best Practices for Implementing SOAP Services

When implementing SOAP services, it is important to follow best practices to ensure that the service is secure, reliable, and maintainable. Here are some best practices for implementing SOAP services:

1. Use HTTPS for communication: HTTPS provides encryption and authentication for SOAP messages, ensuring that the messages cannot be intercepted or modified in transit.
2. Use WS-Security for message-level security: WS-Security provides a standard way to secure SOAP messages, including authentication, encryption, and digital signatures.
3. Use WSDL to define the interface: WSDL provides a standardized way to define the interface of a SOAP service, making it easier for clients to consume the service.
4. Use SOAP Faults for error handling: SOAP Faults provide

a standardized way to handle errors in SOAP services, including error codes and descriptions.

5. Use XML Schema for data validation: XML Schema provides a way to define the structure and content of the data exchanged in SOAP messages, ensuring that the data is valid and consistent.

6. Use versioning to manage changes: Versioning provides a way to manage changes to the interface of a SOAP service, ensuring that existing clients are not broken by changes.

7. Use logging and monitoring for debugging: Logging and monitoring provide a way to debug SOAP services by recording and analyzing SOAP messages and service performance.

By following these best practices, you can ensure that your SOAP services are secure, reliable, and maintainable. In the next section, we will explore the process of testing and debugging SOAP services.

32

Handling Namespaces and Headers

I n SOAP services, namespaces are used to avoid naming
conflicts between elements and attributes in XML
messages. Headers, on the other hand, are used to carry
additional information about the message or its context.

Handling namespaces and headers correctly is important
for ensuring that SOAP services work correctly and can in-
teroperate with clients that use different XML schema and
message formats.

Handling Namespaces

When defining the XML schema for a SOAP service, you can
use namespaces to group related elements and attributes
together and to avoid naming conflicts. However, when using
namespaces in SOAP messages, you need to ensure that the
namespaces are defined correctly and consistently.

In particular, you need to ensure that:

· The namespaces used in the XML schema are correctly reflected in the SOAP messages
· The prefixes used for the namespaces are consistent throughout the SOAP message
· The namespaces used for elements and attributes are defined consistently throughout the SOAP message

To handle namespaces correctly in SOAP services, you can use tools and frameworks that provide support for XML schema and SOAP messaging, such as JAX-WS, Apache Axis2, and .NET Web Services.

Here is an example of how namespaces are used in a SOAP message:

```
<soap:Envelope
xmlns:soap="http://www.w3.org/2003/05/soap-envelope/"
            xmlns:ns1="http://example.com">
  <soap:Header>
    <ns1:authentication>
      <ns1:username>user</ns1:username>
      <ns1:password>password</ns1:password>
    </ns1:authentication>
  </soap:Header>
  <soap:Body>
    <ns1:getStockPrice>
      <ns1:symbol>GOOG</ns1:symbol>
    </ns1:getStockPrice>
  </soap:Body>
</soap:Envelope>
```

In this example, the SOAP message uses the "**http://example.com**" namespace for the "authentication", "username", "password", "getStockPrice", and "symbol" elements. The namespace is defined using the "ns1" prefix, which is used consistently throughout the message.

Handling Headers

Headers are used in SOAP messages to carry additional information about the message or its context. For example, headers can be used to provide authentication credentials, transactional information, or message routing information.

To handle headers correctly in SOAP services, you need to ensure that:

- The headers are defined correctly in the XML schema for the service
- The headers are added to the SOAP message using the correct namespace and element name
- The headers are processed correctly by the service and any intermediate nodes

To handle headers correctly in SOAP services, you can use tools and frameworks that provide support for SOAP messaging, such as JAX-WS, Apache Axis2, and .NET Web Services.

Here is an example of how headers are used in a SOAP message:

```
<soap:Envelope
xmlns:soap="http://www.w3.org/2003/05/soap-envelope/"
                xmlns:ns1="http://example.com">
  <soap:Header>
    <ns1:authentication>
      <ns1:username>user</ns1:username>
      <ns1:password>password</ns1:password>
    </ns1:authentication>
    <ns1:transaction>
      <ns1:id>123456</ns1:id>
      <ns1:timestamp>2023-04-20T12:00:00Z
</ns1:timestamp>
    </ns1:transaction>
  </soap:Header>
  <soap:Body>
    <ns1:getStockPrice>
      <ns1:symbol>GOOG</ns1:symbol>
    </ns1:getStockPrice>
  </soap:Body>
</soap:Envelope>
```

In this example, the SOAP message includes two headers: "authentication" and "transaction". The headers are defined in the "**http://example.com**" namespace and use the "ns1" prefix. The "authentication" header includes a "username" and "password" element, while the "transaction" header includes an "id" and "timestamp" element.

By including these headers in the SOAP message, the client is able to provide authentication and transactional information to the service. The service can then use this information to process the request and provide a response.

33

API Authentication and Authorization

Authentication and authorization are essential components of any API, including SOAP APIs. API authentication is the process of verifying the identity of the client that's making the request. Authorization, on the other hand, determines whether the client is allowed to access the requested resource or perform the requested operation. In this section, we'll explore the different types of authentication and authorization methods that can be used in SOAP APIs.

Basic Authentication

Basic authentication is the most commonly used method of authentication in SOAP APIs. In this method, the client includes a username and password in the HTTP header of the request. The server verifies the credentials and grants access to the requested resource if the credentials are valid.

While basic authentication is simple to implement, it has some drawbacks. For example, the credentials are sent in plaintext, making it vulnerable to interception and eavesdropping. It's recommended to use HTTPS when implementing basic authentication to secure the transmission of credentials.

WS-Security

WS-Security is a widely adopted standard for securing SOAP messages. It provides a framework for adding security to SOAP messages by defining security headers and policies. WS-Security supports a range of security mechanisms, including message encryption, digital signatures, and username tokens.

In WS-Security, the client includes security tokens in the message header to authenticate and authorize the request. The server verifies the tokens and grants access to the resource if the tokens are valid.

OAuth

OAuth is an open standard for secure API authentication and authorization. It's widely used in RESTful APIs, but can also be used in SOAP APIs. In OAuth, the client obtains an access token from an authorization server by presenting credentials. The client includes the access token in the request to authenticate and authorize the request.

OAuth is a flexible and secure method of authentication and authorization that allows clients to access protected resources without disclosing their credentials.

SAML

Security Assertion Markup Language (SAML) is an XML-based standard for exchanging authentication and authorization data between parties. SAML provides a framework for describing and exchanging security-related information, such as authentication and authorization data.

In SAML, the client obtains a SAML assertion from an identity provider. The client includes the SAML assertion in the SOAP message header to authenticate and authorize the request. The server verifies the assertion and grants access to the resource if the assertion is valid.

Mutual Authentication

Mutual authentication is a method of authentication that requires both the client and the server to authenticate each other. In this method, the client presents its credentials to the server, and the server presents its credentials to the client. This provides a higher level of security than basic authentication, as it ensures that both parties are authenticated.

In mutual authentication, SSL/TLS is used to secure the

communication between the client and the server. The client and the server both have a digital certificate that includes a public key. The client and the server verify each other's digital certificates to ensure that they're communicating with the correct party.

Conclusion:

In conclusion, API authentication and authorization are essential components of any SOAP API. There are different methods of authentication and authorization that can be used in SOAP APIs, each with its own advantages and disadvantages. It's important to choose the method that best fits your API's requirements and to implement it correctly to ensure the security and integrity of your SOAP API.

34

Error Handling and Faults

Introduction to Error Handling and Faults

E rror handling and fault handling are crucial aspects of building a SOAP API. An error occurs when a client sends an invalid request to the server, while a fault occurs when an error occurs on the server-side. Faults are standardized error messages in SOAP APIs that provide information about the error and how it can be resolved.

Correct error handling and fault handling are essential for the success of SOAP APIs. Poor error handling and fault handling can lead to frustrated users and reduced API usage. It is also important to ensure that error messages and fault messages are clear and concise, so that users can quickly and easily understand the issue and take the necessary steps to resolve it.

SOAP Faults

SOAP faults are a standard way of reporting errors and faults in SOAP messages. A SOAP fault message contains a faultcode, a faultstring, and an optional faultactor. The faultcode identifies the type of fault, while the faultstring provides a description of the fault. The faultactor identifies the node that caused the fault.

There are several common types of SOAP faults, including "ClientFault," "ServerFault," and "VersionMismatch." A ClientFault occurs when the client sends an invalid request to the server, while a ServerFault occurs when an error occurs on the server-side. A VersionMismatch fault occurs when the version of the SOAP message is not compatible with the server.

To handle SOAP faults in client applications, developers should use try-catch blocks to catch SOAP exceptions. The catch block should then extract the fault information from the exception and handle it appropriately. In server applications, developers should generate SOAP fault messages using the appropriate SOAP fault codes and messages.

Error Handling Best Practices

To ensure that SOAP APIs provide a good user experience, developers should follow some best practices for error handling and fault handling. First, error messages and fault messages should be designed to be clear and helpful to users. Error messages should provide enough information for users to understand the issue and take the necessary steps to resolve it.

Second, error handling should be consistent and predictable across all API methods. The same error codes and messages should be used consistently across all API methods. Developers should also ensure that the API methods return appropriate HTTP status codes to indicate the result of the API call.

Third, developers should log and monitor errors and faults in SOAP APIs. This can help developers to identify common issues and improve the API over time. Developers should also consider implementing automated error reporting, which can help to quickly identify and resolve errors.

Examples of Error Handling and Faults in SOAP APIs

To illustrate best practices for error handling and fault handling in SOAP APIs, let's consider some real-world examples. For example, let's say that a SOAP API for a banking system receives an invalid account number from a client. The API

243

should return an appropriate SOAP fault message with a "ClientFault" code and a message that describes the issue. The message should also provide guidance on how to resolve the issue.

Another example is a SOAP API for a flight reservation system. If the client sends an invalid date for a flight reservation, the API should return a SOAP fault message with a "ClientFault" code and a message that provides details on the error. The message should also provide guidance on how to correctly format the date.

Conclusion

In conclusion, error handling and fault handling are critical aspects of building a SOAP API. SOAP faults provide a standard way of reporting errors and faults in SOAP messages, while clear and concise error messages and fault messages help users to quickly understand and resolve issues. By following best practices for error handling and fault handling, developers can ensure that their SOAP APIs provide a good user experience and are reliable and consistent. Logging and monitoring errors and faults can also help developers to improve the API over time and provide a better user experience.

Implementing error handling and fault handling in SOAP APIs can be complex, but following best practices and using standardized fault codes and messages can help to ensure that the API is easy to use and maintain. By prioritizing error handling and fault handling, developers can create SOAP APIs that are more usable, reliable, and effective.

35

Testing and Debugging

Introduction to Testing and Debugging

Testing and debugging are essential steps in building a SOAP API. Testing ensures that the API functions as expected and meets the requirements, while debugging helps to identify and resolve any issues that arise during development.

Effective testing and debugging can help to improve the quality and reliability of a SOAP API. It can also help developers to identify issues early in the development process and avoid costly errors and delays.

Types of Testing

There are several types of testing that developers can use to ensure the quality and reliability of a SOAP API. These include:

Unit Testing: Unit testing involves testing individual components of the API, such as methods or functions, in isolation. This can help to identify issues early in the development process and ensure that each component functions correctly.

Integration Testing: Integration testing involves testing how different components of the API work together. This can help to identify issues that may arise when components are combined and ensure that the API functions correctly as a whole.

System Testing: System testing involves testing the API as a whole, including its interactions with external systems and databases. This can help to ensure that the API meets the requirements and functions correctly in a production environment.

Performance Testing: Performance testing involves testing the API's performance under different conditions, such as high load or concurrent users. This can help to identify performance bottlenecks and ensure that the API can handle the expected traffic.

Debugging Techniques

When issues arise during the development process, developers must use effective debugging techniques to identify and resolve them. Some common debugging techniques include:

Logging: Developers can use logging to record information about the API's behavior, such as requests and responses. This can help to identify issues and provide information for debugging.

Debugging Tools: Developers can use debugging tools, such as integrated development environments (IDEs) and debuggers, to identify issues and step through code to identify the root cause of issues.

Reproduction: Developers can attempt to reproduce the issue in a controlled environment, such as a test environment, to identify the root cause of the issue.

Best Practices for Testing and Debugging

To ensure that SOAP APIs are tested and debugged effectively, developers should follow some best practices. First, developers should ensure that testing is automated where possible. This can help to identify issues quickly and ensure that testing is consistent across all components of the API.

Second, developers should use test data that reflects real-world scenarios. This can help to identify issues that may not arise in a controlled testing environment.

Third, developers should prioritize testing and debugging throughout the development process. This can help to identify issues early and avoid costly errors later in the development process.

Conclusion

In conclusion, testing and debugging are essential aspects of building a SOAP API. Effective testing and debugging can help to improve the quality and reliability of the API, and identify issues early in the development process. By using effective testing techniques and prioritizing debugging, developers can ensure that their SOAP APIs meet the requirements and function correctly in production environments.

VI

API Consumption

36

API Client Libraries

Introduction to API Client Libraries

A PI client libraries are software libraries that help developers to consume APIs by providing an easy-to-use interface to interact with the API. Client libraries abstract away the complexity of the API, making it easier for developers to use and integrate the API into their applications.

Client libraries are available for a wide range of programming languages and frameworks, including popular languages such as Python, JavaScript, and Java. Using a client library can help to speed up development time and reduce the complexity of interacting with an API.

Benefits of Using API Client Libraries

There are several benefits to using API client libraries, including:

Reduced Complexity: Client libraries abstract away the complexity of the API, making it easier for developers to use and integrate the API into their applications.

Faster Development: Using a client library can help to speed up development time by providing pre-built code for interacting with the API.

Consistency: Client libraries provide a consistent interface for interacting with the API, making it easier to maintain and update code over time.

Improved Error Handling: Client libraries can handle errors and exceptions in a consistent way, making it easier for developers to handle errors and provide feedback to users.

Choosing an API Client Library

When choosing an API client library, developers should consider several factors, including:

Language Support: Developers should choose a client library that supports the programming language they are using for their application.

Documentation: The client library should have clear and comprehensive documentation to help developers get started quickly and troubleshoot any issues.

Community Support: Developers should choose a client library with an active and supportive community, as this can help to ensure that the library is maintained and updated over time.

Features and Functionality: The client library should have the necessary features and functionality to interact with the API in the way that is required by the application.

Implementing an API Client Library

When implementing an API client library, developers should follow best practices to ensure that the library is easy to use and maintain over time. These best practices include:

Keeping it Simple: The client library should be easy to use and understand, with a simple and intuitive interface.

Consistent Design: The client library should have a consistent design and interface, making it easier for developers to use and maintain over time.

Error Handling: The client library should handle errors and exceptions in a consistent and user-friendly way, providing helpful feedback to users.

Documentation: The client library should have clear and comprehensive documentation, making it easy for developers to get started and troubleshoot issues.

Conclusion

In conclusion, API client libraries can help to make consuming

APIs easier and faster, by abstracting away the complexity of the API and providing a simple and consistent interface. When choosing and implementing a client library, developers should consider factors such as language support, documentation, community support, and features and functionality. By following best practices, developers can ensure that their client library is easy to use and maintain over time.

37

Making API Requests

Introduction to Making API Requests

aking API requests is the process of sending requests to an API in order to retrieve or manipulate data. API requests can be made using a variety of tools, including command-line tools, web-based tools, and programming languages.

To make an API request, a developer must first identify the API endpoint they wish to interact with, and then send a request to that endpoint using the appropriate HTTP method.

Anatomy of an API Request

An API request consists of several components, including:

API Endpoint: The URL of the API endpoint that the request is being sent to.

HTTP Method: The HTTP method used for the request, such as GET, POST, PUT, or DELETE.

Request Headers: Headers that provide additional information about the request, such as authentication information, content type, or caching information.

Request Body: The data being sent with the request, if any.

Making API Requests using cURL

cURL is a command-line tool that can be used to make API requests. To make a request using cURL, a developer must specify the API endpoint, the HTTP method, and any necessary request headers or data.

Here's an example of a cURL request:

bashCopy code

curl -X GET https://api.example.com/users -H "Authorization: Bearer <token>"

In this example, the developer is making a GET request to the **/users** endpoint of the **api.example.com** API, and including an authentication token in the request headers.

Making API Requests using JavaScript

In JavaScript, developers can use the built-in **fetch** API to make API requests. To make a request using **fetch**, a developer must specify the API endpoint, the HTTP method, and any necessary request headers or data.

Here's an example of a **fetch** request:

```
fetch('https://api.example.com/users', {
  method: 'GET',
  headers: {
    'Authorization': 'Bearer <token>'
  }
})
  .then(response => response.json())
  .then(data => console.log(data))
  .catch(error => console.error(error));
```

In this example, the developer is making a GET request to the **/users** endpoint of the **api.example.com** API, and including an authentication token in the request headers. The response is then converted to JSON and logged to the console.

Handling API Responses

When making API requests, developers must also handle the responses returned by the API. API responses typically include a status code, response headers, and a response body containing the requested data.

Developers must also handle errors and exceptions that may occur during the request process. This can include network errors, invalid requests, or errors returned by the API itself.

Conclusion

In conclusion, making API requests is a critical part of consuming APIs. Developers must be able to identify the API endpoint they wish to interact with, and then send requests using the appropriate HTTP method, headers, and data. API responses must also be handled carefully, including status codes, response headers, and response data. By understanding how to make API requests, developers can effectively consume APIs and build powerful applications.

38

Handling API Responses

Introduction to Handling API Responses

When making API requests, developers must also handle the responses returned by the API. API responses typically include a status code, response headers, and a response body containing the requested data.

Handling API responses involves parsing the response data, checking for errors and exceptions, and transforming the response into a format that can be used by the application.

Parsing Response Data

API response data can be returned in a variety of formats, including JSON, XML, or CSV. Developers must be able to parse the response data into a usable format, such as an array or object.

In JavaScript, the **JSON.parse()** method can be used to

convert JSON response data into a JavaScript object. Similarly, XML response data can be parsed using XML parsers such as **xml2js**.

Here's an example of parsing JSON response data in JavaScript:

```
fetch('https://api.example.com/users')
  .then(response => response.json())
  .then(data => {
    // Do something with the data
  })
  .catch(error => console.error(error));
```

In this example, the **response.json()** method is used to parse the JSON response data returned by the API.

Checking for Errors and Exceptions

API responses can include errors and exceptions that must be handled by the application. These can include network errors, server errors, or user errors such as invalid input.

Developers must be able to check for these errors and exceptions and respond appropriately. This can include displaying error messages to the user, retrying failed requests, or logging errors for debugging purposes.

Here's an example of handling errors in a JavaScript fetch request:

```
fetch('https://api.example.com/users')
  .then(response => {
    if (!response.ok) {
      throw new Error('Network response was not
```

```
    ok');
  }
  return response.json();
})
.then(data => {
  // Do something with the data
})
.catch(error => console.error(error));
```

In this example, the **response.ok** property is used to check for network errors, and an error is thrown if the response is not ok.

Transforming the Response

API responses can be transformed into a format that is more usable by the application. This can include formatting dates, converting units of measurement, or merging data from multiple responses.

Developers must be able to transform API responses in a way that makes sense for the application. This can include using helper libraries or writing custom transformation functions.

Here's an example of transforming API response data in JavaScript:

```
fetch('https://api.example.com/users')
  .then(response => response.json())
  .then(data => {
    const transformedData = data.map(user => {
      return {
        id: user.id,
        name: `${user.first_name}
```

```
      ${user.last_name}`,
      email: user.email.toLowerCase()
    };
  });
  // Do something with the transformed data
})
.catch(error => console.error(error));
```

In this example, the API response data is transformed into a new object that includes the user's ID, full name, and lowercase email address.

Conclusion

In conclusion, handling API responses is a critical part of consuming APIs. Developers must be able to parse response data into a usable format, check for errors and exceptions, and transform the response into a format that makes sense for the application. By understanding how to handle API responses, developers can effectively consume APIs and build powerful applications.

39

Error Handling and Retries

Introduction to Error Handling and Retries

When consuming APIs, errors and failures are inevitable. These can be caused by a variety of factors such as network issues, server errors, rate limiting, or incorrect user input.

To provide a better user experience, it's important to handle these errors gracefully and provide users with clear feedback. In addition, retrying failed requests can help increase the reliability and performance of the application.

Handling Errors

When an error occurs during an API request, it's important to handle it gracefully and provide the user with clear feedback. This can include displaying error messages or dialogs that explain what went wrong and how to fix it.

It's also important to log errors for debugging purposes.

This can help developers identify and fix issues with the application or the API.

Retrying Failed Requests

In some cases, retrying failed API requests can help increase the reliability and performance of the application. This is especially useful when dealing with transient errors such as network timeouts or rate limiting.

When retrying failed requests, it's important to have a strategy in place to avoid overwhelming the API or causing other issues. This can include implementing exponential backoff or limiting the number of retries.

Implementing Error Handling and Retries

There are many libraries and tools available for implementing error handling and retries in API consumption. These can range from simple helper functions to full-fledged libraries that handle all aspects of error handling and retries.

Here's an example of implementing error handling and retries in JavaScript using the **axios** library:

```
const axios = require('axios');

axios.get('https://api.example.com/users')
  .then(response => {
    // Do something with the response
  })
  .catch(error => {
    console.error(error);
    if (error.response) {
```

```
// Handle known errors
switch (error.response.status) {
  case 401:
    // Unauthorized
    break;
  case 404:
    // Not found
    break;
  // Handle other status codes
  default:
    // Retry the request
    axios.get('https://api.example.com/users')
      .then(response => {
        // Do something with the response
      })
      .catch(error => {
        console.error(error);
        // Handle the error
      });
    break;
}
} else {
  // Retry the request
  axios.get('https://api.example.com/users')
    .then(response => {
      // Do something with the response
    })
    .catch(error => {
      console.error(error);
      // Handle the error
    });
}
});
```

In this example, **axios** is used to make an API request. If
an error occurs, the error is logged to the console and the

appropriate action is taken based on the error type.

If the error is a known error such as a 401 or 404 status code, it is handled accordingly. If the error is not a known error, the request is retried.

Conclusion

In conclusion, handling errors and retries is an important part of consuming APIs. By handling errors gracefully and retrying failed requests, developers can provide a better user experience and increase the reliability and performance of the application. By using the right tools and libraries, developers can simplify the process of implementing error handling and retries and focus on building great applications.

40

Rate Limiting and Throttling

Introduction to Rate Limiting and Throttling

API providers often impose rate limits and throttling to prevent abuse and ensure fair usage of their services. Rate limiting limits the number of requests a user can make over a certain time period, while throttling limits the rate at which requests can be made.

When consuming APIs, it's important to respect these limits and handle rate limiting and throttling errors gracefully.

Rate Limiting

API providers may impose rate limits to prevent users from overwhelming their services. Rate limits can be enforced on a per-user basis or across all users.

To handle rate limiting, it's important to keep track of the number of requests made and respect the limits imposed by the API provider. When a rate limit is reached, the API provider may return a 429 Too Many Requests status code or another error indicating that the rate limit has been exceeded.

To prevent hitting rate limits, it's important to use efficient code and avoid making unnecessary API requests. Caching responses can also help reduce the number of API requests made.

Throttling

Throttling limits the rate at which requests can be made to an API. This can be used to prevent abuse or to ensure fair usage of the API.

Throttling can be enforced by delaying requests or by limiting the number of requests that can be made within a certain time period. When throttling is in effect, the API provider may return a 429 Too Many Requests status code or another error indicating that the request has been throttled.

To handle throttling, it's important to respect the limits imposed by the API provider and avoid making requests at a higher rate than allowed. Implementing exponential backoff can also help prevent hitting throttling limits.

Implementing Rate Limiting and Throttling

There are many libraries and tools available for implementing rate limiting and throttling in API consumption. These can range from simple helper functions to full-fledged libraries that handle all aspects of rate limiting and throttling.

Here's an example of implementing rate limiting and throttling in Python using the **ratelimit** library:

```
from ratelimit import limits, sleep_and_retry
import requests

@sleep_and_retry
@limits(calls=10, period=60)
def make_api_request():
    response =
    requests.get('https://api.example.com/users')
    if response.status_code == 429:
        raise Exception('Rate limit exceeded')
    response.raise_for_status()
    return response.json()

try:
    response = make_api_request()
    # Do something with the response
except Exception as e:
    print(e)
    # Handle the error
```

In this example, the **make_api_request** function is deco-
rated with the **sleep_and_retry** and **limits** decorators. The
sleep_and_retry decorator adds a delay between retries,
while the **limits** decorator enforces a rate limit of 10 requests
per minute.

If the rate limit is exceeded, an exception is raised and
caught in the **try** block. The exception can be handled by
logging the error or retrying the request after a certain amount
of time.

Conclusion

In conclusion, rate limiting and throttling are important

concepts to consider when consuming APIs. By respecting the limits imposed by the API provider and handling rate limiting and throttling errors gracefully, developers can provide a better user experience and avoid hitting API limits. By using the right tools and libraries, developers can simplify the process of implementing rate limiting and throttling and focus on building great applications.

41

Caching API Responses

Introduction to Caching API Responses

C aching API responses can significantly improve the performance and reduce the load on API servers. By caching responses, subsequent requests for the same data can be served from the cache instead of making new API requests.

When consuming APIs, it's important to understand the caching mechanisms available and use them to improve performance.

Types of Caching

There are several types of caching mechanisms available for API responses, including:

- Client-side caching: This involves caching responses on the client side, such as in a web browser's cache or a mobile app's local storage.

- Server-side caching: This involves caching responses on the server side, such as in a caching layer or a database.
- Content delivery networks (CDNs): CDNs are a type of server-side caching that cache responses on multiple geographically distributed servers to improve performance and reduce latency.

Implementing Caching

To implement caching in API consumption, it's important to understand the caching mechanisms available and choose the appropriate one for the use case.

For client-side caching, web browsers and mobile apps typically have built-in caching mechanisms that can be used to cache API responses. By setting appropriate caching headers in API responses, developers can control how long responses are cached and when they should be invalidated.

For server-side caching, there are several caching solutions available, including in-memory caches like Redis, distributed caches like Memcached, and caching layers like Varnish. By configuring these caches to store API responses and setting appropriate expiration times, developers can improve performance and reduce the load on API servers.

CDNs can also be used to cache API responses and improve performance. By configuring a CDN to cache responses from an API endpoint, subsequent requests for the same data can be served from the CDN cache instead of making new API requests.

Cache Invalidation

One challenge with caching API responses is cache invalidation. When data changes on the server, cached responses may become stale and outdated. To prevent serving stale data, it's important to implement cache invalidation mechanisms that ensure that cached responses are invalidated when the underlying data changes.

One approach to cache invalidation is to use a time-based expiration mechanism, where cached responses are invalidated after a certain amount of time. Another approach is to use a cache invalidation mechanism that invalidates the cache when the underlying data changes.

Conclusion

In conclusion, caching API responses is an important technique for improving performance and reducing the load on API servers. By understanding the caching mechanisms available and implementing appropriate caching solutions, developers can provide a better user experience and reduce the load on API servers. By implementing cache invalidation mechanisms, developers can ensure that cached responses are always up-to-date and avoid serving stale data.

42

Best Practices for API Consumption

Introduction to Best Practices for API Consumption

When consuming APIs, it's important to follow best practices to ensure that the API is used effectively and efficiently. Best practices help developers to build robust, reliable, and scalable applications that provide a good user experience.

Use API Clients and Libraries

API clients and libraries can help to simplify API consumption by providing a high-level interface for making API requests and handling responses. These libraries often abstract away the details of making HTTP requests and parsing responses, allowing developers to focus on building their application logic.

Using API clients and libraries can also help to ensure that best practices are followed for making API requests, such as adding appropriate headers, handling errors, and managing retries.

Handle Errors and Exceptions

When consuming APIs, errors and ex

ceptions can occur for various reasons, such as network issues, API rate limiting, or invalid API requests. It's important to handle these errors and exceptions gracefully to ensure that the application provides a good user experience.

One way to handle errors and exceptions is to use try-catch blocks to handle exceptions that may occur during API consumption. Another way is to use error handling libraries or frameworks that provide a unified way of handling errors across different APIs.

Implement Rate Limiting and Throttling

APIs may impose rate limiting and throttling to prevent abuse and ensure fair usage. When consuming APIs, it's important to implement rate limiting and throttling mechanisms to ensure that API requests are made within the allowed limits.

One way to implement rate limiting and throttling is to use a library or framework that provides these features out-of-the-box. Another way is to implement custom rate limiting and throttling logic based on the API provider's guidelines.

Use Caching to Improve Performance

Caching API responses can significantly improve the performance of API consumption by reducing the number of API requests and improving response times. When consuming APIs, it's important to use caching mechanisms to improve performance and reduce the load on API servers.

There are several types of caching mechanisms available, including client-side caching, server-side caching, and content delivery networks (CDNs). By using appropriate caching mechanisms, developers can improve performance and reduce the load on API servers.

Follow API Documentation and Guidelines

API providers often provide documentation and guidelines for consuming their APIs. It's important to follow these guidelines to ensure that API consumption is done effectively and efficiently.

API documentation often provides information on how to authenticate, make API requests, handle errors, and implement best practices. By following API documentation and guidelines, developers can avoid common pitfalls and ensure that their application works correctly with the API.

Conclusion

In conclusion, following best practices for API consumption is important for building robust, reliable, and scalable applications that provide a good user experience. By using API clients and libraries, handling errors and exceptions, implementing rate limiting and throttling, using caching to improve performance, and following API documentation and guidelines, developers can ensure that their application works effectively and efficiently with the API.

VII

API Testing and Monitoring

43

Types of API Tests

Introduction to API Testing and Monitoring

API testing and monitoring are critical components of API development that ensure that APIs are reliable, scalable, and provide a good user experience. Testing and monitoring help to identify issues before they impact users and ensure that APIs are performing as expected.

Types of API Tests

There are several types of API tests that can be performed to ensure that APIs are functioning as expected. These tests include:

- Unit Tests: These tests focus on testing individual components of an API, such as functions, methods, or classes. Unit tests help to ensure that each component of the API works correctly and as intended.

- Integration Tests: These tests focus on testing how different components of the API work together. Integration tests help to ensure that the API works as a cohesive whole and that there are no issues when different components are used together.
- Functional Tests: These tests focus on testing the functionality of the API as a whole, such as making API requests and verifying that the expected responses are returned. Functional tests help to ensure that the API works as intended from an end-user perspective.
- Performance Tests: These tests focus on testing the performance of the API, such as the response times, throughput, and resource utilization. Performance tests help to ensure that the API can handle expected levels of traffic and that there are no performance issues.
- Security Tests: These tests focus on testing the security of the API, such as testing for vulnerabilities, authentication, and authorization. Security tests help to ensure that the API is secure and protected from potential attacks.

API Monitoring

API monitoring is the process of continuously monitoring APIs to ensure that they are performing as expected and to identify issues as they arise. API monitoring involves monitoring various metrics, such as response times, error rates, and resource utilization, to ensure that the API is functioning correctly.

API monitoring can be performed using various tools and services that provide real-time monitoring and alerting capabilities. These tools can help to identify issues before they impact users and ensure that the API is performing as expected.

Conclusion

In conclusion, API testing and monitoring are critical components of API development that ensure that APIs are reliable, scalable, and provide a good user experience. By performing various types of API tests, such as unit tests, integration tests, functional tests, performance tests, and security tests, developers can ensure that their API works as intended and is secure. By monitoring APIs in real-time, developers can identify issues before they impact users and ensure that the API is performing as expected.

44

Testing Tools and Frameworks

Introduction to Testing Tools and Frameworks

T here are several testing tools and frameworks available that can be used to test and monitor APIs. These tools and frameworks provide various capabilities for testing, such as automated testing, load testing, security testing, and performance testing.

Popular Testing Tools and Frameworks

Some popular testing tools and frameworks for API testing and monitoring include:

- Postman: Postman is a popular API development and testing tool that provides capabilities for testing APIs, creating and sharing API documentation, and monitoring APIs.
- SoapUI: SoapUI is an open-source testing tool that pro-

vides capabilities for testing SOAP and REST APIs. SoapUI supports various types of API testing, such as functional testing, load testing, and security testing.

- JMeter: JMeter is an open-source load testing tool that can be used to test the performance and scalability of APIs. JMeter supports various protocols, including HTTP, HTTPS, and SOAP.
- Newman: Newman is a command-line tool that allows developers to run Postman collections in a CI/CD pipeline. Newman provides capabilities for automated testing, integration testing, and load testing.
- Assertible: Assertible is a testing and monitoring tool that provides capabilities for API testing, automated testing, and continuous monitoring. Assertible supports various types of API tests, such as functional testing, performance testing, and security testing.

Choosing the Right Testing Tool or Framework

When choosing a testing tool or framework for API testing and monitoring, it's important to consider factors such as the type of API being tested, the level of testing required, and the budget.

For example, if the API being tested is a REST API, then a tool such as Postman or Newman may be a good fit for functional testing and integration testing. If load testing is required, then JMeter may be a better fit.

It's also important to consider the ease of use and learning curve of the tool or framework, as well as the level of support and community around the tool or framework.

Conclusion

In conclusion, there are several testing tools and frameworks available for API testing and monitoring, each with its own capabilities and strengths. By choosing the right tool or framework for the type of API being tested and the level of testing required, developers can ensure that their APIs are reliable, scalable, and provide a good user experience.

45

Writing Test Cases and Test Suites

Introduction to Writing Test Cases and Test Suites

In API testing and monitoring, writing test cases and test suites is an important part of ensuring the reliability and functionality of an API. Test cases and test suites can help identify issues and errors in the API, and can also help developers ensure that the API meets the requirements and specifications.

Best Practices for Writing Test Cases and Test Suites

When writing test cases and test suites for API testing and monitoring, it's important to follow best practices to ensure that the tests are effective and efficient. Some best practices for writing test cases and test suites include:

- Clearly define the test cases and test suites: Test cases and test suites should be clearly defined and documented to ensure that they are repeatable and can be easily understood by other developers.

- Cover all aspects of the API: Test cases and test suites should cover all aspects of the API, including functionality, performance, security, and error handling.

- Use automation tools: Automation tools such as Postman or Newman can help automate the testing process and ensure that the tests are repeatable and consistent.

- Use realistic data: Test cases and test suites should use realistic data to ensure that the API behaves as expected under real-world conditions.

- Prioritize tests: Test cases and test suites should be prioritized based on the importance of the functionality being tested and the likelihood of errors occurring.

Writing Test Cases

When writing test cases for API testing and monitoring, it's important to consider the following:

- Define the test scenario: The test scenario should clearly define the inputs, expected outputs, and steps for executing the test.

- Use a structured approach: Test cases should be written using a structured approach, such as Arrange-Act-Assert (AAA) or Given-When-Then, to ensure that the test is consistent and repeatable.

- Use realistic data: Test cases should use realistic data to ensure that the API behaves as expected under real-world conditions.

Writing Test Suites

When writing test suites for API testing and monitoring, it's important to consider the following:

- Group related test cases: Test cases should be grouped together based on their functionality or the area of the API being tested.
- Prioritize tests: Test suites should prioritize tests based on the importance of the functionality being tested and the likelihood of errors occurring.
- Use automation tools: Automation tools such as Postman or Newman can help automate the testing process and ensure that the tests are repeatable and consistent.

Conclusion

In conclusion, writing test cases and test suites is an important part of API testing and monitoring. By following best practices for writing test cases and test suites, developers can ensure that their APIs are reliable, functional, and meet the requirements and specifications.

46

Mocking and Stubbing

Introduction to Mocking and Stubbing

I n API testing and monitoring, mocking and stubbing are techniques used to simulate the behavior of an API that is not yet implemented or not yet available for testing. By simulating the API behavior, developers can test their applications and ensure that they are functioning correctly even if the API is not yet available.

Mocking vs Stubbing

Mocking and stubbing are similar techniques, but they are used in different contexts.

- Mocking: Mocking is used to create a fake implemen-tation of an API, allowing developers to test their ap-plications without relying on the actual API. Mocking is typically used in the early stages of development when the actual API is not yet available or is still being developed.
- Stubbing: Stubbing is used to simulate the behavior of an API that is not yet available for testing. Stubs are typically created based on the API specifications or documentation and are used to test the application's interactions with the API.

Benefits of Mocking and Stubbing

Using mocking and stubbing in API testing and monitoring offers several benefits, including:

- Testing without dependencies: Mocking and stubbing allow developers to test their applications without relying on the actual API or other external dependencies.
- Early detection of issues: By testing the application with mocks and stubs, developers can detect issues and errors early in the development process, when they are easier and less expensive to fix.
- More efficient testing: Mocking and stubbing allow for more efficient testing, as developers can test specific scenarios without needing to run the entire application.

Best Practices for Mocking and Stubbing

When using mocking and stubbing in API testing and monitoring, it's important to follow best practices to ensure that the tests are effective and efficient. Some best practices for mocking and stubbing include:

- Use real API specifications: Stubs should be created based on the real API specifications or documentation to ensure that they accurately simulate the behavior of the API.
- Focus on key scenarios: Stubs should focus on key scenarios and interactions with the API, rather than trying to simulate every possible scenario.
- Update stubs as needed: Stubs should be updated as the API specifications or documentation changes to ensure that they accurately reflect the behavior of the API.
- Use automation tools: Automation tools such as Postman or Newman can help automate the creation and use of stubs, making the testing process more efficient.

Conclusion

In conclusion, mocking and stubbing are valuable techniques in API testing and monitoring, allowing developers to test their applications without relying on the actual API or other external dependencies. By following best practices for mocking and stubbing, developers can ensure that their tests are effective and efficient, leading to more reliable and functional applications.

47

Continuous Integration and Deployment

Introduction to Continuous Integration and Deployment

Continuous integration and deployment (CI/CD) is a set of practices and tools that enable teams to automate the process of building, testing, and deploying software. CI/CD helps teams to deliver software more quickly and reliably, and can be particularly useful in the context of API testing and monitoring.

Benefits of CI/CD for API Testing and Monitoring

Using CI/CD in API testing and monitoring offers several benefits, including:

- Faster feedback: CI/CD enables teams to quickly test and deploy changes to the API, allowing for faster feedback on the quality of the changes.
- More reliable tests: By automating the testing process, CI/CD helps to ensure that tests are executed consistently and accurately, leading to more reliable and effective tests.
- Increased efficiency: CI/CD automates many of the repetitive and time-consuming tasks associated with testing and deployment, allowing teams to focus on higher-level tasks and more strategic work.

Best Practices for CI/CD in API Testing and Monitoring

When using CI/CD in API testing and monitoring, it's important to follow best practices to ensure that the process is effective and efficient. Some best practices for CI/CD in API testing and monitoring include:

- Automate as much as possible: The more that can be automated, the more efficient the process will be. This includes automating testing, building, and deployment processes.
- Use version control: Version control is critical for managing changes to the API and ensuring that changes can be tracked and rolled back if necessary.
- Use containers: Containers, such as Docker, can help to ensure consistency and portability across different

environments.

· Monitor and log: Monitoring and logging can help to identify issues and errors, and can provide valuable insights into the behavior of the API.

Conclusion

In conclusion, CI/CD is a valuable set of practices and tools for API testing and monitoring, enabling teams to automate the process of building, testing, and deploying software. By following best practices for CI/CD in API testing and monitoring, teams can ensure that the process is effective and efficient, leading to more reliable and functional APIs.

48

API Monitoring and Alerting

Introduction to API Monitoring and Alerting

API monitoring and alerting is the process of continuously monitoring an API's availability, performance,
and functionality, and sending alerts if issues are
detected. This is a critical component of API testing and
monitoring, as it enables teams to quickly identify and
respond to issues that can impact the API's usability and
reliability.

Benefits of API Monitoring and Alerting

Using API monitoring and alerting offers several benefits,
including:

- Early detection of issues: Monitoring an API allows teams
to detect issues early, before they impact users or cause
significant downtime.

- Improved reliability: By continuously monitoring an API, teams can ensure that it remains reliable and functional, and can quickly respond to any issues that arise.
- Better user experience: Monitoring an API can help to identify issues that impact the user experience, enabling teams to improve the API's usability and performance.

Best Practices for API Monitoring and Alerting

When implementing API monitoring and alerting, it's important to follow best practices to ensure that the process is effective and efficient. Some best practices for API monitoring and alerting include:

- Define metrics and thresholds: Define metrics, such as response time and error rates, and set thresholds for acceptable levels of performance. Use these metrics to trigger alerts when thresholds are exceeded.
- Monitor from multiple locations: Monitor an API from multiple locations to ensure that it is available and functional from different geographic regions.
- Use synthetic testing: Use synthetic testing to simulate user interactions with the API, and monitor the API's response to these interactions.
- Implement automated alerting: Implement automated alerting to ensure that issues are quickly identified and addressed.

Conclusion

In conclusion, API monitoring and alerting is a critical component of API testing and monitoring, enabling teams to continuously monitor an API's availability, performance, and functionality, and quickly respond to any issues that arise. By following best practices for API monitoring and alerting, teams can ensure that their APIs remain reliable, functional, and provide a positive user experience.

49

Performance and Load Testing

Introduction to Performance and Load Testing

Performance and load testing are critical components of API testing and monitoring, as they help to ensure that APIs can handle a high volume of traffic and maintain acceptable levels of performance. Performance testing is the process of measuring an API's response time, throughput, and resource utilization under normal operating conditions, while load testing is the process of measuring an API's performance under heavy traffic loads.

Benefits of Performance and Load Testing

Using performance and load testing offers several benefits, including:

- Identifying bottlenecks: Performance and load testing can help to identify bottlenecks and other issues that

impact an API's performance.
- Improving scalability: By identifying bottlenecks and other issues, performance and load testing can help to improve an API's scalability and ability to handle high volumes of traffic.
- Enhancing reliability: Performance and load testing can help to identify issues that impact an API's reliability, enabling teams to address these issues and improve the API's overall functionality.

Best Practices for Performance and Load Testing

When implementing performance and load testing for APIs, it's important to follow best practices to ensure that the testing process is effective and efficient. Some best practices for performance and load testing include:

- Define realistic test scenarios: Define test scenarios that accurately simulate real-world usage of the API.
- Use realistic test data: Use realistic test data to ensure that test results accurately reflect the API's performance under real-world conditions.
- Monitor system resources: Monitor system resources during testing to identify any issues related to resource utilization.
- Use automated tools: Use automated testing tools to reduce the time and effort required for testing and to ensure consistent results.

Conclusion

In conclusion, performance and load testing are critical components of API testing and monitoring, enabling teams to identify bottlenecks, improve scalability, and enhance reliability. By following best practices for performance and load testing, teams can ensure that their APIs perform optimally under normal and heavy traffic loads, and provide a positive user experience.

VIII

API Security

50

Common API Security Threats

Introduction to Common API Security Threats

A PI security threats are a serious concern for organizations that use APIs to share data and services. A successful API attack can result in the theft of sensitive data, disruption of services, and damage to an organization's reputation. Understanding common API security threats is crucial for building secure APIs that can protect against these threats.

Common API Security Threats

The following are some of the most common API security threats that organizations face:

- Authentication and Authorization Attacks: These attacks aim to exploit vulnerabilities in the authentication and authorization processes of an API, such as brute force attacks, session hijacking, and token theft.

- Injection Attacks: These attacks involve injecting malicious code or data into an API request to exploit vulnerabilities in the API's data processing functions, such as SQL injection, XML injection, and command injection.
- Cross-Site Scripting (XSS): XSS attacks exploit vulnerabilities in an API's web application to inject malicious code into a user's browser, potentially allowing an attacker to steal sensitive information.
- Cross-Site Request Forgery (CSRF): CSRF attacks trick users into executing malicious actions on an API by using a trusted user's identity.
- Man-in-the-Middle (MitM) Attacks: MitM attacks involve intercepting communications between an API and its users to steal sensitive data or modify the data exchanged.
- Denial of Service (DoS) and Distributed Denial of Service (DDoS) Attacks: These attacks aim to overwhelm an API with traffic, preventing legitimate users from accessing the API's services.

Mitigating Common API Security Threats

To mitigate common API security threats, organizations can implement several security measures, including:

- Authentication and Authorization: Use secure authentication and authorization methods, such as multi-factor authentication and token-based authorization.
- Input Validation: Validate all user input to prevent injection attacks, such as SQL injection and XML injection.

- Output Encoding: Encode output data to prevent XSS attacks.
- CSRF Protection: Use CSRF protection methods, such as CSRF tokens and same-site cookies.
- Transport Layer Security (TLS): Use TLS encryption to protect API traffic from MitM attacks.
- Rate Limiting: Implement rate limiting to prevent DoS and DDoS attacks.

Conclusion

In conclusion, API security threats can have serious consequences for organizations that use APIs to share data and services. Understanding common API security threats and implementing appropriate security measures can help to protect APIs from these threats and ensure the security and integrity of API data and services.

51

Authentication Mechanisms

Authentication is the process of verifying the identity of a user or a system. In the context of APIs, authentication is essential to ensure that only authorized parties can access protected resources.

There are several authentication mechanisms available for API security, each with its strengths and weaknesses. Some of the commonly used authentication mechanisms are:

1. API keys: An API key is a unique identifier that is used to authenticate API requests. API keys are often used to rate-limit requests and control access to specific resources.

2. OAuth2: OAuth2 is a widely adopted protocol that allows third-party applications to access protected resources on behalf of a user. OAuth2 uses access tokens to authenticate API requests.

3. JSON Web Tokens (JWT): A JWT is a compact, URL-safe means of representing claims to be transferred between two parties. JWTs are often used for authentication and

authorization purposes.

4. Basic authentication: Basic authentication is a simple authentication mechanism that uses a username and password to authenticate API requests. While basic authentication is easy to implement, it is not very secure as the username and password are transmitted in plain text.

5. Digest authentication: Digest authentication is an improved version of basic authentication that uses a hashed password instead of transmitting the password in plain text. While digest authentication is more secure than basic authentication, it is not as widely adopted.

6. Client certificates: Client certificates are a type of digital certificate that are used to authenticate clients to servers. Client certificates are often used in situations where a higher level of security is required.

It is important to choose the right authentication mechanism based on your specific security requirements. Additionally, it is recommended to use HTTPS to encrypt all API requests and responses to prevent eavesdropping and man-in-the-middle attacks.

API Keys

API keys are a simple authentication mechanism that is widely used in API security. An API key is a unique identifier that is used to authenticate API requests. API keys are often used to rate-limit requests and control access to specific resources.

API keys are easy to implement and do not require complex cryptographic protocols. However, API keys can be easily compromised if they are not kept secure. Therefore, it is recommended to use HTTPS to encrypt all API requests and responses to prevent API key theft.

To use API keys for authentication, the API provider generates a unique API key for each client. The client then includes the API key in each API request as a query parameter or a header. The API provider can then validate the API key to ensure that the request is coming from an authorized client.

API keys can be revoked or regenerated if they are compromised or if the client no longer needs access to the API. It is important to have a process in place to manage API keys and ensure that they are not leaked or stolen.

API keys are suitable for simple authentication scenarios where only a few clients need access to the API. However, for more complex authentication scenarios, such as user authentication, more robust authentication mechanisms such as OAuth2 or JWT should be used.

OAuth 2.0

OAuth 2.0 is an authorization framework that is widely used in API security. It provides a standardized way for clients to access resources on behalf of users. OAuth 2.0 is a flexible and extensible framework that can be used for a wide range of authentication and authorization scenarios.

OAuth 2.0 consists of several components, including clients, resource servers, authorization servers, and resource owners. Clients are applications that want to access protected resources on behalf of a user. Resource servers are servers that host protected resources. Authorization servers are servers that issue access tokens to clients after a user grants permission. Resource owners are users who have access to protected resources.

OAuth 2.0 uses access tokens to grant clients access to protected resources. Access tokens are short-lived tokens that are issued by the authorization server after the user grants permission. The client then includes the access token in each API request as a query parameter or a header. The resource server can then validate the access token to ensure that the request is coming from an authorized client.

OAuth 2.0 provides several different grant types that are used to obtain access tokens. The most common grant types are the authorization code grant type and the client credentials grant type. The authorization code grant type is used for web applications and requires the user to interact with a web page to grant permission. The client credentials grant type is used for server-to-server communication and does not require user interaction.

OAuth 2.0 is a widely adopted standard and is supported by many API providers and client libraries. However, OAuth 2.0 can be complex to implement and can be prone to security vulnerabilities if implemented incorrectly. Therefore, it is important to follow best practices when implementing OAuth 2.0, such as using HTTPS to encrypt all communication, validating redirect URIs, and using secure storage for access tokens.

JWT

JSON Web Tokens (JWTs) is a token-based authentication mechanism that allows secure transmission of information between parties as a JSON object. A JWT consists of three parts: a header, a payload, and a signature.

The header contains metadata about the token such as the algorithm used for signing it. The payload contains claims or statements about the user or entity being authenticated, which can include user ID, email, and other data. The signature is generated by combining the header and payload with a secret key using a specific algorithm, which ensures the integrity of the JWT and prevents tampering.

JWTs are often used in web applications and APIs as a way of authenticating and authorizing users without the need for server-side storage of session data. The user logs in once and receives a JWT that is then sent with each subsequent request, allowing the server to authenticate and authorize the user without needing to store session data.

One of the benefits of JWTs is their self-contained nature, as the token contains all the information needed for authentication and authorization. This makes JWTs portable and easy to use across different systems and platforms.

However, JWTs must be stored securely, as anyone with access to a JWT can potentially use it to gain access to protected resources. Additionally, JWTs have a limited lifespan, and should be invalidated and refreshed periodically to prevent unauthorized access.

52

Role-based Access Control

Role-based access control (RBAC) is a security mechanism that provides access to resources based on the roles assigned to users or entities. In RBAC, permissions are assigned to roles, and roles are assigned to users or groups. This allows administrators to manage access to resources based on the responsibilities and roles of users, rather than assigning permissions directly to individual users.

RBAC is a popular mechanism for managing access to APIs, as it allows fine-grained control over access to resources. This can help prevent unauthorized access to sensitive data or operations, and can also make it easier to manage access permissions as users come and go.

RBAC can be implemented in different ways, depending on the specific needs of an API. One common approach is to define a set of roles that correspond to different levels of access, such as "admin", "editor", and "viewer". Permissions are then assigned to each role, specifying the actions that users with that role are allowed to perform.

When a user makes a request to the API, the system checks

the user's assigned roles and permissions to determine whether the requested operation is allowed. If the user has the required role and permissions, the request is granted; otherwise, it is denied.

RBAC can be a powerful tool for managing access to APIs, but it requires careful planning and management to ensure that permissions are assigned correctly and users are properly authenticated and authorized. It is important to regularly review and update role assignments to ensure that they accurately reflect the current needs and responsibilities of users.

53

Input Validation and Sanitization

Input validation and sanitization are important techniques for preventing attacks that exploit vulnerabilities in API inputs, such as injection attacks, cross-site scripting (XSS), and buffer overflow attacks. These attacks can be used to gain unauthorized access to systems or data, modify or delete data, or disrupt API operations.

Input validation is the process of verifying that the input received by an API conforms to expected standards, such as length, format, and data type. This helps to prevent attacks that exploit vulnerabilities in input fields, such as SQL injection, cross-site scripting (XSS), and buffer overflow attacks.

Sanitization is the process of removing or encoding malicious or unwanted characters and input from API requests. This can be done by removing characters that are not allowed, encoding special characters to prevent injection attacks, and filtering out inputs that are not needed or that contain sensitive information.

To implement input validation and sanitization, it is important to have a clear understanding of the expected input types and formats for each API endpoint, and to implement appropriate validation and sanitization methods for each input field. This can be done using tools and frameworks such as regular expressions, input validation libraries, and web application firewalls.

It is also important to regularly test the input validation and sanitization mechanisms to ensure that they are effective and that they are able to prevent common attacks. This can be done using tools such as vulnerability scanners, penetration testing, and security audits.

Overall, input validation and sanitization are critical components of API security, and they should be implemented carefully and rigorously to ensure that APIs are protected from attacks and vulnerabilities.

54

Rate Limiting and Quotas

A nother important aspect of API security is rate limiting and quotas. These mechanisms allow you to limit the number of requests that can be made to your API within a certain time frame, which can help prevent abuse and overloading of your system.

Rate limiting typically involves setting a maximum number of requests that can be made per user or per IP address, and enforcing this limit by either blocking or throttling requests that exceed it. Throttling involves delaying requests that exceed the limit, rather than blocking them outright.

Quotas are similar to rate limiting, but instead of limiting the number of requests, they limit the amount of data that can be transferred. This can be useful for controlling costs, as well as preventing abuse.

To implement rate limiting and quotas, you will need to track the usage of your API, typically by logging requests and their associated metadata (e.g. user or IP address). You can then use this information to enforce your limits and prevent abuse.

There are a number of third-party tools and services that can help you implement rate limiting and quotas, such as API management platforms and cloud service providers. Alternatively, you can build your own custom solution using libraries and frameworks that provide rate limiting and quota management functionality.

It's important to strike a balance between security and usability when implementing rate limiting and quotas. You don't want to make it too difficult for legitimate users to access your API, but at the same time, you need to prevent abuse and protect your system from overload.

55

HTTPS

HTTPS (Hypertext Transfer Protocol Secure) is a protocol for secure communication over the internet. It is used to encrypt the data that is transmitted between the client and the server, which helps to prevent eavesdropping, tampering, and other security threats.

Using HTTPS for API communication is strongly recommended to ensure that sensitive data such as login credentials, personal information, or financial data is transmitted securely. It is also necessary for complying with various security and privacy regulations.

HTTPS works by encrypting the data using Transport Layer Security (TLS) or Secure Sockets Layer (SSL) protocols. This encryption ensures that the data cannot be read or modified by anyone who intercepts it during transmission. In addition, HTTPS uses digital certificates to verify the identity of the server, which helps to prevent man-in-the-middle attacks.

To implement HTTPS for an API, the server must have an SSL/TLS certificate installed, which is used to encrypt the data.

The certificate is issued by a trusted certificate authority (CA) and contains information about the identity of the server.

Developers should also ensure that clients are configured to use HTTPS by default, and that they validate the server's certificate to prevent man-in-the-middle attacks. They should also monitor and renew SSL/TLS certificates as necessary, and keep up with industry best practices to ensure the security of their API.

Overall, using HTTPS is an essential step in securing API communication and protecting sensitive data from security threats.

IX

API Documentation and Developer Experience

56

Importance of Good Documentation

Good documentation is essential for any successful API. It's a critical component of the developer experience, as it provides developers with the necessary information to effectively use and integrate the API into their projects. Proper documentation helps to avoid confusion, misunderstandings, and errors. Without it, developers may struggle to understand how the API works, leading to frustration and wasted time.

Good documentation is also essential for attracting and retaining developers. If an API is difficult to use, developers are likely to seek out alternatives that are more straightforward and easier to work with. On the other hand, clear and comprehensive documentation can make an API more appealing to developers, leading to increased adoption and usage.

In the following sections, we'll dive deeper into the different aspects of API documentation and best practices for creating a great developer experience.

57

API Documentation Types

There are several different types of documentation that are important to include in API documentation:

- **Getting Started:** This type of documentation is aimed at helping new developers get up and running quickly with the API. It should include information on how to obtain an API key or token, how to authenticate with the API, and how to make basic requests.
  - **Reference Documentation:** This type of documentation provides detailed information on the API's endpoints, parameters, and responses. It should include examples of request and response payloads, as well as information on error codes and messages.
  - **Tutorials and Guides:** These are step-by-step instructions on how to use the API to accomplish specific tasks. They should include real-world use cases and examples.
  - **API Status and Changelog:** This documentation

provides information on the current status of the API and any recent updates or changes.

58

Best Practices for API Documentation

reating effective API documentation requires careful attention to detail and a focus on the developer experience. Here are some best practices to keep in mind:

- **Make it easy to find:** Ensure that your documentation is easy to navigate and find what developers are looking for. A clear table of contents and search functionality can help with this.
- **Provide clear examples:** Use real-world examples to illustrate how the API works and how to use it in practice. Including code snippets and sample requests and responses can be especially helpful.
- **Be consistent:** Use consistent language and formatting throughout your documentation. This can help to avoid confusion and make it easier for developers to quickly find the information they need.
- **Keep it up to date:** Ensure that your documentation is accurate and up to date with the latest API changes and

updates.

- **Solicit feedback:** Encourage developers to provide feedback on your documentation and take their suggestions into account when making updates and improvements.

59

Developer Experience

In addition to providing good documentation, creating a great developer experience involves several other factors, including:

- **Ease of use:** Ensure that your API is easy to use and integrate into existing projects. This can involve providing clear error messages, consistent response formats, and easy-to-use SDKs.
- **Support and community:** Providing good support and fostering a strong developer community can help to build a loyal user base and encourage developers to continue using and promoting your API.
- **Consistency:** Consistency is key when it comes to creating a good developer experience. Ensure that your API follows established conventions and best practices, and avoid unnecessary complexity or confusion.
- **Feedback and iteration:** Continuously gathering feedback from developers and iterating on your API based on that feedback can help to improve the developer experience

over time.

60

Documenting API Endpoints

I n this section, we will discuss the best practices for documenting API endpoints. A well-documented API makes it easier for developers to understand how to use it, which can save time and reduce the risk of errors. Here are some tips for documenting API endpoints:

1. Use clear and concise language: Avoid using technical jargon or overly complex language. Use simple language and provide clear examples to make it easier for developers to understand.
2. Include all relevant information: Document all the input parameters, output data, and any relevant information about the endpoint, such as expected response codes.
3. Use consistent formatting: Use a consistent format for documenting each endpoint. This can include a brief summary, the HTTP method used, the URL of the endpoint, and the request and response parameters.
4. Provide examples: Providing examples of how to use the endpoint can be helpful for developers. This can include

sample requests and responses in various formats, such as JSON or XML.

5. Update documentation regularly: As the API evolves and changes over time, make sure to update the documentation to reflect those changes.

6. Provide a searchable index: A searchable index of all endpoints can make it easier for developers to find the information they need.

7. Make the documentation accessible: Ensure that the documentation is easy to access and available in multiple formats, such as HTML, PDF, or online help.

By following these best practices, you can create well-documented API endpoints that are easy for developers to use and understand.

61

Interactive Documentation Tools

In addition to traditional documentation, interactive documentation tools can be incredibly helpful for developers. These tools provide an easy-to-use interface that allows developers to explore an API's endpoints and parameters in a more visual way. Some popular interactive documentation tools include:

1. Swagger UI: Swagger UI is an open-source tool that generates an interactive API documentation website from an OpenAPI specification. It allows developers to test API endpoints directly from the documentation and even generate sample code snippets in a variety of programming languages.

2. Postman: Postman is a popular tool used for API development and testing, but it also includes a feature for generating API documentation. The tool allows developers to create detailed documentation for their API endpoints, including parameters, examples, and response codes.

3. ReDoc: ReDoc is an open-source tool that generates API documentation from an OpenAPI specification. It provides a clean and simple interface that is easy to navigate and understand.

4. Stoplight: Stoplight is a tool that allows developers to design, document, and test APIs all in one place. It includes an interactive documentation feature that allows developers to test endpoints and generate code snippets directly from the documentation.

5. Apiary: Apiary is a tool that helps teams design, document, and test APIs. It includes an interactive documentation feature that allows developers to test endpoints and generate code snippets directly from the documentation.

Using an interactive documentation tool can greatly improve the developer experience by making it easier to explore and understand an API's functionality. These tools can also help to reduce the time and effort required for developers to integrate an API into their applications.

Swagger/OpenAPI

Swagger/OpenAPI is a popular interactive documentation tool used for documenting RESTful APIs. It allows developers to easily discover and understand the API's capabilities by providing a visual representation of the API endpoints, parameters, and response data.

The Swagger/OpenAPI specification is a machine-readable format that defines the structure and functionality of an API. It uses JSON or YAML to describe the API endpoints, request and response data, security mechanisms, and other metadata.

One of the key benefits of using Swagger/OpenAPI is that it allows developers to generate client code and server stubs for multiple programming languages, which helps to speed up development and improve code quality. Additionally, Swagger/OpenAPI provides a unified way to document RESTful APIs, which makes it easier for developers to understand and work with different APIs.

There are several tools available for creating and managing Swagger/OpenAPI documentation, including Swagger Editor, Swagger UI, and Redoc. These tools provide a user-friendly interface for editing and viewing Swagger/OpenAPI documentation, and can be used to generate API client libraries and server stubs.

Overall, using Swagger/OpenAPI for documenting RESTful APIs can help to improve the developer experience and make it easier for developers to build high-quality applications. By providing a clear and consistent way to document APIs, Swagger/OpenAPI can reduce the time and effort required to integrate with third-party APIs and improve the overall reliability and security of API-based applications.

RAML

RAML (RESTful API Modeling Language) is another popular tool used for creating interactive API documentation. It allows developers to design, document, and test their APIs in an easy and efficient way.

RAML is based on the YAML (YAML Ain't Markup Language) format, which is a human-readable data serialization language. This makes it easy for developers to write and understand the API documentation.

One of the key features of RAML is its ability to generate client code in multiple programming languages based on the API documentation. This helps developers to quickly create client-side applications that can consume the API.

RAML also supports versioning of APIs, which allows developers to make changes to the API without breaking existing client applications. It also provides support for security, such as OAuth 2.0 and API keys, as well as rate limiting and throttling.

Overall, RAML is a powerful tool for creating interactive API documentation and can help improve the developer experience when working with APIs.

Apiary/Blueprint

Apiary is a web-based platform for designing, documenting, and testing APIs. It provides a collaborative interface for API design, with built-in support for the OpenAPI (formerly known as Swagger) and API Blueprint formats.

API Blueprint is a high-level description format for REST APIs, with a simple syntax that allows developers to describe the resources, requests, and responses of an API in a concise and human-readable way. Apiary provides a visual editor for API Blueprint, making it easy to create and maintain documentation.

With Apiary, developers can create interactive documentation that allows users to try out API endpoints and see the responses in real-time. This can help to reduce the learning curve for new users, and provide a more engaging experience overall.

Apiary also includes features for automated testing and validation of API endpoints, making it easier to ensure that the API is functioning as expected. The platform integrates with popular testing frameworks like Postman and Newman, allowing developers to easily run tests and get feedback on their API.

Overall, Apiary is a powerful tool for creating comprehensive API documentation that is easy to use and maintain. Its support for the API Blueprint format, along with its built-in testing and validation features, make it a popular choice among developers and API providers.

62

SDKs and Client Libraries

SDKs (Software Development Kits) and client libraries are an essential part of a developer's toolkit. They provide pre-built code and tools to make it easier for developers to consume APIs, speeding up the development process and reducing the chance of errors.

When building an API, it's important to provide SDKs and client libraries for popular programming languages to make it easier for developers to integrate with your API. These libraries should include easy-to-use interfaces, clear documentation, and examples to help developers get started.

There are many SDKs and client libraries available for various programming languages, including Java, Python, Ruby, and JavaScript. Many API management platforms, such as Amazon API Gateway and Google Cloud Endpoints, also provide tools to generate SDKs and client libraries for your API automatically.

When providing SDKs and client libraries, it's important to keep them up to date with the latest changes to your API. This ensures that developers have access to the latest features and bug fixes and helps to maintain a positive developer experience.

63

Versioning and Deprecation Strategies

I n API development, versioning is crucial to ensure that API clients and applications can maintain compatibility and functionality even as changes are made to the API. It involves creating and managing multiple versions of the same API. This allows developers to introduce new features or make changes to the API without disrupting existing clients. Versioning can be done in several ways, including:

1. URI versioning: This involves adding a version number to the URI of the API, such as example.com/api/v1.
2. Query parameter versioning: This involves adding a version number as a query parameter in the URL, such as example.com/api?version=1.
3. Header versioning: This involves adding a version number as a custom header in the HTTP request.

When deciding on a versioning strategy, it's essential to consider factors such as how often changes are made to the API, how significant those changes are, and how they will impact existing clients.

Another critical aspect of versioning is deprecation. As APIs evolve and new versions are released, older versions may need to be deprecated or phased out. Deprecation involves marking a version as obsolete and encouraging developers to upgrade to a newer version. It's essential to communicate deprecation clearly to API users, provide ample notice and support during the transition period, and offer alternatives for deprecated functionality.

Overall, having a well-thought-out versioning and deprecation strategy is critical to ensure the smooth and successful evolution of an API over time.

64

Providing Code Examples

In addition to providing comprehensive documentation, code examples can be incredibly helpful to developers looking to use an API. Code examples can be included in documentation or provided as a separate resource.

When creating code examples, it's important to keep in mind the intended audience and provide examples in multiple programming languages, if possible. This will help developers who may be using a different programming language than what was used to develop the API.

Code examples should also be well-documented, with clear explanations of what each line of code does. This will help developers understand how to use the code and modify it to fit their specific needs.

In addition to traditional code examples, it can be helpful to provide sample projects or starter kits that developers can use as a starting point for their own projects. This can save time and make it easier for developers to get started using the API.

When making changes to an API, it's important to update

all associated code examples and sample projects to reflect the changes. This will ensure that developers have the most up-to-date information and examples to work with.

Overall, providing clear and comprehensive code examples can greatly improve the developer experience when using an API.

65

Building and Supporting a Developer Community

In addition to providing clear and comprehensive documentation, building and supporting a developer community can greatly improve the developer experience when working with an API. A strong developer community can help answer questions, provide feedback, and promote the API to others who may be interested.

There are several strategies that can be used to build and support a developer community, such as:

1. Creating a forum or message board where developers can ask and answer questions, share tips and best practices, and engage with other members of the community.

2. Hosting regular webinars or live streams that cover topics related to the API, such as new features or use cases.

3. Organizing hackathons or developer events that allow developers to showcase their projects and collaborate with others.

4. Encouraging developers to share their feedback and suggestions for improving the API.
5. Providing resources such as tutorials, sample code, and documentation to help developers get started with the API.
6. Offering incentives such as rewards or recognition for developers who make significant contributions to the community.

By building and supporting a strong developer community, API providers can create a more engaging and supportive environment for developers to work in, leading to increased adoption and usage of the API.

X

Scaling and Optimizing APIs

66

Identifying API Performance Bottlenecks

As the popularity of an API increases, so does the volume of requests it receives. This can lead to performance bottlenecks that impact the API's overall performance and reliability. To identify these bottlenecks, it is important to monitor key metrics and analyze the data to identify patterns and trends.

One key metric to monitor is response time, which is the amount of time it takes for the API to respond to a request. High response times can be an indicator of performance issues such as slow database queries or inefficient code. Another important metric is throughput, which is the number of requests the API can handle per second. When throughput reaches its limit, it can lead to slow response times or even API crashes.

API logs can provide valuable insights into the performance of the API. These logs should capture key metrics such as response time, throughput, and error rates. Analyzing these logs can help identify patterns and trends, such as high volume of requests during certain times of day or specific endpoints that are causing performance issues.

Load testing can also be used to identify performance bottlenecks. By simulating a large number of requests, load testing can help identify the maximum capacity of the API and any performance issues that arise under heavy load.

Once performance bottlenecks have been identified, there are several strategies that can be used to optimize API performance:

1. Caching: Caching frequently accessed data can significantly reduce response times and improve throughput.
2. Scaling: Scaling horizontally by adding more servers or vertically by upgrading hardware can increase the API's capacity to handle requests.
3. Load balancing: Distributing requests across multiple servers can improve throughput and prevent any single server from becoming overloaded.
4. Code optimization: Optimizing code by identifying and removing inefficiencies can improve response times and reduce the load on servers.

By monitoring key metrics, analyzing data, and implementing optimization strategies, API developers can ensure their APIs perform optimally even under heavy load.

67

Load Balancing and Clustering

Load balancing and clustering are essential strategies for scaling and optimizing APIs. Load balancing involves distributing incoming requests evenly across multiple servers to prevent any one server from being overloaded with requests. Clustering, on the other hand, involves grouping multiple servers together to work as a single unit. Together, load balancing and clustering help improve the performance and reliability of APIs, ensuring they can handle large volumes of traffic and provide a high-quality user experience.

One popular load balancing technique is round-robin, where incoming requests are distributed evenly across all available servers in a circular fashion. This ensures that no server is overworked, and all servers have an equal opportunity to handle incoming requests. Another technique is called sticky sessions, where incoming requests are directed to the same server that initially handled the request. This technique is useful when handling stateful requests where session information needs to be maintained between requests.

Clustering involves grouping multiple servers together to work as a single unit. This can be achieved using different techniques, such as master-slave, where one server acts as the master and coordinates all requests, while the others act as slaves and handle the actual processing. Another technique is called peer-to-peer, where all servers in the cluster work together as equals, sharing the workload and coordinating requests between themselves.

Both load balancing and clustering can be implemented using a variety of tools and technologies, such as NGINX, HAProxy, and Kubernetes. These tools provide easy-to-use interfaces for configuring and managing load balancing and clustering, allowing API developers to focus on building their APIs rather than worrying about the underlying infrastructure.

In addition to load balancing and clustering, there are other strategies that can be used to optimize API performance, such as caching, compression, and content delivery networks (CDNs). Caching involves storing frequently accessed data in memory or on disk, reducing the number of requests that need to be processed by the API. Compression involves reducing the size of data being transmitted over the network, reducing network bandwidth usage and improving API response times. CDNs involve distributing content across a network of servers around the world, allowing users to access content from a server closer to their physical location, reducing network latency and improving performance.

By implementing these strategies, API developers can ensure that their APIs are scalable, reliable, and optimized for performance, providing a high-quality user experience to their users.

68

Caching Strategies

C aching is one of the most effective ways to improve the performance and scalability of an API. By caching responses to frequently requested API calls, you can reduce the number of requests your server needs to process, resulting in faster response times and reduced server load.

There are several different caching strategies you can use for your API, depending on your specific requirements:

1. Client-side caching: This strategy involves caching responses on the client-side, such as in the browser's cache or a mobile app's local storage. This can reduce the number of requests sent to the server and improve the app's performance. However, it is important to consider the expiration time of the cached data and ensure that it is refreshed periodically to avoid serving stale data.

2. Server-side caching: This strategy involves caching responses on the server-side, such as in a cache layer or a content delivery network (CDN). This can help reduce the load on the backend server and improve response

times. However, it is important to consider the cache invalidation strategy, so that users are served up-to-date data.

3. Content-based caching: This strategy involves caching responses based on the content of the request. For example, if a request includes a certain query parameter or a certain value in the request body, the response can be cached for that specific request. This can help reduce the number of cache misses and improve response times.

4. Edge caching: This strategy involves caching responses at the edge of the network, such as in a CDN. This can help reduce the load on the backend servers and improve response times for users located far from the origin servers.

When implementing a caching strategy for your API, it is important to consider the cache invalidation strategy, expiration time, and the potential impact on data consistency. It's also important to test and monitor the caching strategy to ensure that it is effective and not causing any unintended consequences.

69

Server-side Caching

Server-side caching is one of the most effective strategies for optimizing API performance. It involves caching the response of a request on the server-side so that subsequent requests for the same resource can be served directly from the cache. This reduces the number of database queries and network requests required to generate the response, resulting in faster response times and lower server load.

There are several different types of server-side caching strategies that can be used, including:

1. In-memory caching: In-memory caching involves storing the cached data in the server's RAM, which allows for extremely fast access times. This type of caching is best suited for data that is frequently accessed and doesn't change very often.
2. Database caching: Database caching involves storing the cached data in a separate database table, which is faster to access than the main database. This type of caching

is best suited for data that is accessed frequently but changes infrequently.

3. Content Delivery Network (CDN) caching: CDN caching involves caching the response of an API request on a global network of servers. This allows for faster response times and lower server load, particularly for API requests that are made from different geographic locations.

The choice of caching strategy will depend on the specific needs of the API and the performance characteristics of the underlying infrastructure. However, implementing server-side caching is generally considered to be a best practice for optimizing API performance.

70

Client-side Caching

C lient-side caching is another approach to improve the performance of APIs. It involves storing frequently requested data on the client-side, such as in the browser, to avoid making multiple requests to the server.

Client-side caching can be implemented using various techniques, such as browser caching, session storage, and local storage. Browser caching is the most common approach, which involves caching HTTP responses on the client-side. When the user makes a request for the same resource, the browser serves it from the cache instead of requesting it again from the server. This reduces the load on the server and improves the response time.

Session storage and local storage are other client-side caching techniques. Session storage is a temporary storage mechanism that stores data for a particular session, while local storage is a more permanent storage mechanism that stores data until it is explicitly deleted. These mechanisms can be used to cache data that is required frequently, such as user preferences, to avoid making multiple requests to the server.

While client-side caching can improve the performance of APIs, it is important to use it judiciously. Caching too much data can result in increased memory usage, and caching data for too long can result in stale data being served to users. Therefore, it is important to implement caching strategies that strike a balance between performance and data freshness.

71

API Gateway and Backend for Frontend (BFF) Patterns

API Gateway and Backend for Frontend (BFF) patterns are popular approaches to building and scaling APIs. An API Gateway acts as a single entry point for clients to access multiple APIs, providing a centralized location for authentication, authorization, and other cross-cutting concerns. It can also implement caching and rate limiting, as well as handle load balancing and failover to improve availability and performance.

The Backend for Frontend pattern involves building a separate API for each client or front-end application. This allows for better control over the data and functionality that each client requires, as well as improved performance and scalability. Each BFF API can also implement caching, rate limiting, and other optimizations tailored to the specific client.

Both the API Gateway and BFF patterns can be used together to provide a comprehensive solution for scaling and optimizing APIs.

72

Throttling and Rate Limiting

Throttling and rate limiting are important concepts when it comes to scaling and optimizing APIs. Throttling refers to the process of limiting the number of requests per unit of time from a client or set of clients, in order to prevent overload of the API server. This can be useful for controlling traffic spikes and ensuring that the API remains responsive even during periods of high demand.

Rate limiting, on the other hand, is a mechanism for controlling the amount of data that can be transmitted over a network or API in a given period of time. Rate limiting can be used to limit the amount of data that a client can access at any given time, and can be an effective way to prevent abusive behavior, such as DDoS attacks or spamming of an API.

There are several ways to implement throttling and rate limiting in an API. One common approach is to use token buckets, which allow a certain number of requests to be made within a given time period, with tokens being replenished over time. Another approach is to use sliding windows, which allow a certain number of requests to be made within a given time window, after which requests are blocked until the window resets.

It's important to note that throttling and rate limiting can have a significant impact on the user experience of an API, so it's important to carefully consider the trade-offs between security and usability when implementing these measures. In some cases, it may be appropriate to implement more flexible rate limiting policies, such as allowing users to purchase additional API calls or offering different tiers of service depending on usage.

73

Microservices and Serverless Architectures

icroservices and serverless architectures have become increasingly popular in recent years, especially for large-scale applications. Microservices is an architectural style that involves breaking up a large application into smaller, independent services, each with its own functionality and communicating with each other through APIs. Serverless architectures, on the other hand, involve deploying individual functions as independent services that are executed only when triggered by an event.

Both of these approaches offer benefits in terms of scalability and flexibility for APIs. With microservices, you can scale individual services up or down as needed, depending on the load they're experiencing. This can help prevent overloading of resources and ensure that the API can handle spikes in traffic.

Similarly, serverless architectures allow for easy scalability as well. Because each function is independent, it can be scaled up or down as needed, based on its specific usage patterns.

This means that you don't have to worry about provisioning servers or other resources in advance, and you only pay for the resources you actually use.

However, microservices and serverless architectures also come with some challenges when it comes to API development and maintenance. With microservices, you need to make sure that each service is designed to communicate effectively with the others, and that there are no data consistency issues between them. With serverless architectures, you need to ensure that your functions are optimized for efficient execution, and that they can handle any necessary security and authentication requirements.

Overall, though, both microservices and serverless architectures offer a lot of potential for scaling and optimizing APIs, and can help ensure that your API can handle the demands of even the most complex and high-traffic applications.

74

Monitoring and Observability

onitoring and observability are critical aspects of
scaling and optimizing APIs. By monitoring and
observing API performance and usage, teams can
identify potential bottlenecks and proactively address issues
before they impact users.

One important aspect of monitoring and observability is
collecting and analyzing metrics. Metrics provide insights
into the performance of an API and can be used to identify
patterns and trends. Common metrics for API monitoring include response time, request rate, error rate, and throughput.
These metrics can be collected and visualized using tools such
as Grafana, Prometheus, and Elasticsearch.

Another important aspect of monitoring and observability is
logging. Logs provide a detailed record of API activity and can
be used to troubleshoot issues and identify potential security
threats. Logs can be collected and analyzed using tools such
as ELK stack, Splunk, and Graylog.

In addition to metrics and logs, distributed tracing is another useful technique for monitoring and observability in

microservices architectures. Distributed tracing allows teams to trace requests as they traverse multiple services and identify potential issues and bottlenecks. Tools such as Jaeger and Zipkin provide distributed tracing capabilities.

To ensure effective monitoring and observability, it is important to establish clear performance targets and service level objectives (SLOs). SLOs define the level of service that is expected from an API and can be used to measure and monitor performance. They should be established in collaboration with stakeholders and based on user needs and expectations.

Finally, it is important to establish a culture of continuous improvement and iteration around monitoring and observability. Teams should regularly review and analyze metrics, logs, and traces to identify areas for improvement and implement changes to improve API performance and user experience.

Contact

In case further assistance is needed, one contact us through e-mail: rebalkaneducation@gmail.com

Thank you for buying this book.

Din Asotić